A Collection of Essays

A Collection of Essays

By

C. Alfie Gill

A COLLECTION OF ESSAYS

iUniverse books may be ordered through booksellers or by contacting:

iUniverse
1663 Liberty Drive
Bloomington, IN 47403
www.iuniverse.com
1-800-Authors (1-800-288-4677)

Because of the dynamic nature of the Internet, any web addresses or links contained in this book may have changed since publication and may no longer be valid. The views expressed in this work are solely those of the author and do not necessarily reflect the views of the publisher, and the publisher hereby disclaims any responsibility for them.

Any people depicted in stock imagery provided by Thinkstock are models, and such images are being used for illustrative purposes only. Certain stock imagery © Thinkstock.

ISBN: 978-1-5320-2284-5 (sc)
ISBN: 978-1-5320-2283-8 (e)

Library of Congress Control Number: 2017906800

Print information available on the last page.

iUniverse rev. date: 08/15/2018

Contents

SECTION IV

SECTION V

SECTION VI

PREFACE

This volume or collection of essays started many years ago in the sunny island of Barbados. I attended Combermere (then, an all boys' secondary school). It was discovered from early that I had a knack for speaking and writing.

I joined the Drama Club and the Speech and Debating Society. As for writing, most of my essays were said to be creative and highly imaginative. Mr. Frank Collymore, then Deputy Head Master and Founder of the renown Caribbean magazine "BIM" encouraged me to develop my writing skills. I became the first student editor of the school magazine "The Combermerian" in the year 1950.

Hence this volume begins with my writings while in high school consisting of: - Poetry, Sports- Reporting and my first published short story- "A trip to Mt. Soufriere."

In the late 1950's I went to London and eight years later to Canada. In both places, I did some writing but little was published. Published were mainly letters to the daily papers including the "Times of London" and the "Toronto Star". I forgot to mention that in the period 1954-1959, I wrote a number of weekly articles in the Barbados Weekly newspaper called "The Torch", using the 'nom de plume' of Young Democrat.

Most of my writings (published and unpublished) were in the U.S.A. The published writings were mainly in Barbados and the U.S.A. In Barbados, the published writings appeared mainly in the two leading newspapers "The Barbados Advocate" and "The Nation Newspaper of Barbados".

In the U.S.A, the published writings appeared mainly in the monthly magazine of the Moravian Church, U.S.A, both in the form of: (1) Submitted Articles and (2) Letters to the Editor.

The remainder of my writings consisted of given speeches, highly credited term papers and ad hoc writings. The published writings cover miscellaneous topics e.g.: - High School Writings Law, Education, Religion and Politics. Prepare yourself for the product of this writing, starting in High School and stretching over sixty years.

ENJOY

DEDICATION

I dedicate this collection of essays to two persons who have meant a great lot to me. One was my late nephew "Charles Anthony (Tony) Richards" who was called to glory at the unbelievable early age of fifteen. He died just (2) days before his sixteenth birthday.

The second person who made a lasting impression on my always evolving life was my late mother, "Emmeline Gertrude Gill" of St. Michael, Barbados.

Tony was an exceptional person good in books, good in sports, good in everything. At the tender age of five, he was being taken to visit an orphanage. He selected one of his new expensive fire-trucks to take as a gift. When it was suggested that he should take one of last year's trucks, his unforgettable reply was, "No, whenever you give something, always give of one of your best.

The second and most influential person in my life was my late and beloved mother. If ever there was a saint who walked this earth, it was my late mom; St. Emmeline Gertrude Gill, who just did not pay lip service to Christianity but always tried to live a Christian life by literally turning the other cheek. By constantly loving God and loving her neighbor as she loved herself.

She instilled love and the highest standards in Tony (nephew), Dolores (sister) and myself. She was a home-grown philosopher, orator and party comedian. Her quotes were precious and unforgettable. Her favorite quotation was "It could be worse". Oh, how true! I used this quotation constantly. It helped me to face every situation with reality, knowing that it could have been worse. Thank you, Mom, for all your pearls of wisdom.

ACKNOWLEDGEMENTS

This book would not have been possible without the great and invaluable help of several persons. Chief among them were the ever-present spirit of my late mom: "Emmeline Gertrude Gill", Claudette Robinson and Ms. Jennifer P. Lumley.

Mother Emmeline has been a permanent part of my life since Xmas night 1989. Daily she inspires and encourages me. She says "You have important work to finish, time is running out. Let's do it. Finish your writing for your first book. Get all the scripts together. Read them, revise them correct them. Get them ready to be printed. Thank you, mom, this is it. Ready, concise, easy and ready for the printer's "ink."

Secondly, Claudette affectionately known as 'Queenie' has played a great part in my life, especially my spiritual life for a long time. She is smart, sensitive, unselfish and generous. She is the kind of friend that anyone would like to have. She knows how to praise, love, inspire and encourage a partner. She repeated that I had a story worth telling and should not give up but to become firm and resolute of purpose and to burn the mid-night oil, the end-result of which would be my first publication called a "Collection Of Essays".

Thirdly, I shall like to pay tribute to the part played by Ms. Jennifer P. Lumley. I met her in 2015 and at a time when I was about to throw in the towel and abandon my dream of having written a book. I met Ms. Lumley who had written a number of books and who had the practical knowledge and experience for which I was looking. Ms. Lumley is a great writer and one who is on the upward path to success. From the beginning, she has been a source of encouragement and a constant motivator to me.

Ms. Lumley, again I thank you and in this small tribute would like you to know that it is because of you and your tireless efforts that this collection of essays will see the light of day.

SECTION I

The Early Days

1. Darkness

Strange waves of darkness flowed o'er us,
Yet darker and darker it grew
And the clatter of a musket stabbed frayed hearts,
While the moon was obscured by drifting belts of cloud.

We waited in darkness with beating hearts,
Yet darker and darker it grew;
And once more the buoyant stars were seen,
While the moon was obscured by drifting belts of cloud.

Suddenly the silence was broken by the shatter of a musket,
Yet darker and darker it grew;
We tumbled into the walls, converging on a temple door,
While the moon was obscured by drifting belts of cloud.

Then the interior was plunged into darkness,
Though later and later it grew;
But the clouds drew away from the moon
And a silver radiance bathed the temple.

C. Gill (5C) (1949)

2. My Garden

In my sad and lonely hours
Then I go among my flowers.
They tell me of the Father's love,
Shining down from heav'n above.

The rose comes first in my esteem
Of all the flowers she is the Queen.
For beauty and sweetness, it's the rose.
But beware her thorns, they'll ruin your clothes.

Then the tall and stately sweet-peas
They are sure to attract the bees,
Lilies, carnations and tuberoses,
They make the most gorgeous posies.

Stephanotis and the honeysuckle vine
All around your fence will twine,
When the flowers all combine
They are as good as any gold mine.

So any time you're feeling blue,
Go in your garden and select a few,
They'll teach you how to rest at ease,
For in your garden there's sure to be peace.

3. Our Beloved Combermere

Combermere for many boys has played a noble part,
And now that they have to depart;
It means leaving a school so dear
And friends genuinely sincere.

All the boys who are leaving here
Will always cherish dear Combermere,
For it was Combermere that fitted them
For the task that laid ahead of them.

Things at all times will not be sweet
In the life that we are going to meet;
Therefore, we should be armed before,
In order to make success quite sure.

In everything you say or do
Remember the School that fashioned you;
And as Combermerians you ought not to stop
Until you have finally reached the top.

C.A. GILL (5C)

4. Boxing Notes - The Combermerian

1950

Boxing this year became an important and interesting branch of sports. Boxing took the form of a competition this year and points were awarded which would enable one of the six Sets to be champion. Set E carried off the Boxing shields. Competition was interesting and lively and wrought many thrills in the ring which was caused by the keenness of the youngsters. This sport drew many strangers to the school and they watched, many breath-taking and fistic bouts between the seniors.

Last year Boxing was introduced but was based on a different system. Last year there were individual prizes and each boxer was only a unit in the competition and not like this year a representative of an organized body which we called a Set. The fighting this year was a little tamer and not once did we have reproduced the temperament as witnessed last year, for example – The Rudder vs. Shepherd fight.

The boys received instructions in Boxing this year and often sparred during these classes. Mr. Bruce St. John through dint and hard work had the boys up to the standard of schoolboy amateurs. The last two weeks of the Term, I was occupied in the competition for the set Boxing Shield. Eliminations for the championships took place the first week and we saw many young and promising boys fighting at their best to reach the finals. The competition for champion for the preparatory forms took place first. These little boys gave some very entertaining bouts. They punched with vigour, hooked with a zeal and then were often knocked down with precision. Division 4 and members of the first and second forms perhaps gave the most ludicrous performances as they ardently fought to reach the finals.

Too many of these defended and in many cases, there were no aggressors, as these chaps seemed to fight some soft rounds. That gave the other judge Marshall, the popular "Darlington" and myself many bad head-aches as to who should be victor. The chaps who found themselves in this category should learn to fight in a more skillful way and not in a dormant powder-puff spirit. Division 3 and many members gave good account of themselves, using their fists to a great advantage to illustrate this. Division two, or should I say the members of many of the fourth forms gave the best performances to me. These were the boys who fought orthodoxically, they took up correct stances and then were engaged in the most fistic bouts of the tournament. Sealy, P.P. and his brother P. Sealy showed good promise. Cutting from a third form and Archer from 4C were to me the most correct and promising schoolboy amateurs. Cutting and the Sealys sometimes spar at the Brighton Sports Club. Division 1 or members of the fifth form were very tame this year, but nevertheless gave a good account of themselves. Shepherd did not reproduce the form shown last year. Reece was champion of Division 1 this year.

Boxing has now been established successfully at the school, and with proper assistance should remain very successful. I hope in future years to hear more of it, and now I wish it a sad adieu and good luck.

C.A.Gill (5C)

5. Cricket Notes - The Combermerian

1949

The performance of the School team during the year was very good when we contrast their play against opposing teams. As was said last year, the experience gained from consistent defeat was very beneficial to the team and enabled them to gain points and thus give up their place at the foot of the cup. The team managed to gain places in the Batting and Bowling analyses at the end of the season. Mr. F. G. Smith, who scored 152 against Lodge, secured the first place in the Batting Analysis for the School. K. A. Branker, skipper of the School team, took 31 wickets at 12.5 each. Mr. H. G. Brewster who also gained a place took 19 at a cost of 15 runs each.

In this publication of the School Magazine, there is a summarized detail of the matches played, with the scores of both teams. Due to the assistance given by the Masters, these results were encouraging and augur well for future seasons.

The second XI secured 15 points including two outright wins. The victims of a good bowling attack were Lodge and Mental Hospital: Lodge was an easy victim and Mental Hospital – a strong contender for the cup – just succumbed to the school team's bowling which included a successful spell by Mr. J. C. L. Drakes. Both teams are to be complimented for their performances.

vs. LODGE

Combermere played Lodge at home for the first match of the season. This match saw the versatile Mr. F. G. (Sleepy) Smith score the first century of the season. The School team ably led by K.A. Branker was saved from an outright defeat due to their keen fielding during those critical moments. They secured 1 point in their first match.

vs. WANDERERS

The team then entertained Wanderers, last season's champions, and were beaten, but in no way disgraced as we did not allow these stalwarts to make very big scores. Mr. Brewster was in good form and secured for himself six wickets in Wanderers' first attempt at the wicket.

vs. EMPIRE

The School team next journey Hall as the guests of Empire and were defeated. In the first innings Knight, O. R. made 47 which was very useful to the small score. In the second innings Mr. Brewster made 37 which was the highest score in the innings. As usual Branker was in good bowling form and bagged 5 for 56.

vs. CARLTON

This time the team was entertained by Carlton at Black Rock. Carlton decided to bat first and declared 283 for 7. Branker took 4 for 89. In their turn at the wicket the school trumped up 109 runs including a well-played 23 by C. M. Dunnah, an opening batsman. The School team then went back to the wicket where they made a small score of 80.

vs. HARRISON COLLEGE

The School team then played Harrison College who were our guests on this occasion. The team decided to take vengeance on their guests for their previous three defeats. The College team was too weak an opponent for us and therefore submitted to a good thrashing which did not result in an outright win for us due to the lack of time. Our team batted fist and piled up the very good score of 181 runs. Of these Branker made a polished 42, Mr. Brewster a delightful 35, Holder an aggressive 33 and Grant N. a very small but a very good stroke player, made a stubborn 22. College in their turn at the wicket failed, being unable to stand up to the bowling of skipper Branker and Mr. Brewster who each captured 4 wickets for 54 and 51 respectively. Our team in their second venture at the wicket made 59 for 8 declared. College then went back to the wicket where they scored 52 for 8 wickets. Branker captured 3 of these for 13.

vs. SPARTAN

A consistent pour of rain did not allow play on the first Saturday. On the following Saturday, Combermere went to the wicket and made 88, including a well-played 31 by Mr. Brewster who had by this time gained public attention with his aggressive medium paced bowling and his solid batting. Spartan, to everybody's surprise, could only raise 118, and thus enabled the School to gain their fifth point.

vs. PICKWICK

In their last match for the season, the School was again defeated. This was due to the unavoidable absence of its key players and to the illness of Mr. Brewster on the last day. The School made 73 and 42 against Pickwick's 175 for 6 declared. Grant and Wilkinson, both small players, were the only batsmen to defy Pickwick's attack. The former being very defensive and executing some delightful strokes on the leg side which pleased the crowd immensely.

C. A. GILL, 5C

6. A Trip To Mt. Soufriere 1949

On Wednesday, August 9, twenty-four Rovers and twelve scouts left for Mt. Soufriere – an extinct volcano in St. Vincent. I took my place among the others in a kind of contraption which the Vincentians call a bus. AT 7:40 a.m. with a gentle northeasterly wind blowing and the sun gently stretching beyond the peaks of the mountain, the bus gave a jerk, then a noisy hoot and we were on our way.

We drove over two hours, taking many numerous turns and bends at a speed of about sixty miles an hour. We were a happy lot, and by singing and making some vicious movements to the latest calypsos we fought to overcome a strangeness that was quickly overcoming us. The breeze was cool, the scenery was picturesque and the enthusiasm was high among us, that was why we had such a happy drive.

We soon left the tar road and made our way through a stone and debris bedecked road that is called River bed. The river is only present during the rainy season and on all other occasions the river bed is used as a means to reach the out parts of the island. The driving became rough and our weight soon began to tell on the half-rotten floor boards of the bus. Amidst cries of joy, astonishment and even fear, the bus continued on that memorable journey; but our ecstasy did not last long as the top of the gear stick came off. We were forced to get out and continue our way on foot for eight miles approximately. With us were two guides, so we did not cherish any sentiments of losing our way. We garbed ourselves for mountaineering and with the imitations of experienced climbers, we set out on what might be, to most of us, one of the most memorable undertakings in our span of life.

At the beginning, the descent was very gentle and our road was along a narrow path which was made by the constant use of hikers and laborers. The scenery at the beginning was most important, taking the form of green foliage. Here we saw the arrowroot growing, bushes of West Indian cures and wild bush with some lovely trees forming the upright decorations. By this time the sun was high in the heavens, pouring down its powerful rays, which only made us very hot and thirsty. Nevertheless, we were still going on slowly but surely. We had to keep in single file due to the narrowness of the path. We were in spirits and used our voices to a great extent to produce some single notes and a singleness in sound which we called singing. The sound echoed for many miles and with the serenity of nature prevailing, we seem to be cherubim of some celestial state. With such an environment, the first few miles did not manage to succumb us with tediousness, therefore we continued walking, with a slip now and then, in the highest spirits. We photographed much of the scenery around us which was bestowed to us by our loving Father who might have foreseen our pilgrimage to that historic volcano – Soufriere.

Our path soon left the narrow mud path and soaring upward to the left. That began the first part of our rock climbing and here our scenery was changed for the first time. On our left were high mountains; on the right, there was a slight descent with some trees dotted here and there. Before us, mountains seemed to spring up and were soon encompassed by a whiteness that we all knew was a mist. From here, some of our confederates put a length between us and them which we were never able to shorten. We were soon undergoing some alternative points of climbing and falling. The rocks in this area were rough and jagged and we all occasionally got some scrapes and cuts but we did not allow this to daunt our spirits: we continued climbing upward and ever upward. We were soon living one of the most momentous feats in our way; and that was now becoming very humid and we were occasionally having slight showers of rain. We then donned our sweaters, overcoats and other means of warming our bodies; our physical extremities nevertheless, were left exposed to the elements surrounding us, but for obvious reasons we were becoming vary fatigued and were forced to rest, but even after resting, we still felt stiff. It was only a burning desire to see the volcano and our chances to obtain adventure that drove us on. We soon began to despair as we had no water to quench our thirst.

On arriving at a high peak, we saw others forcing on in front of us and with fresh hope, renewed effort and a little humor, we were determined to catch up with the others. Our road again became gentle, but this time the slope was upward and we kept in view, our other comrades. We soon saw them stop and we began to wonder if they were resting or waiting for us. The area now was a broad flat one with no decorations. The air was cold by now and we were all shivering and we wondered how long we would be able to keep it up. We were nearing the others and by now, without knowing it, we were nearing our destination. When we reached the others, we threw ourselves on the ground, never for one moment thinking or being able to guess that we had arrived at Soufriere – our destination.

When I got up and began looking around, I saw a hollow, about a half a mile in diameter and about 500 feet deep with a blue substance in it. On inquiring, I learnt that I was looking at mount Soufriere, The famous West Indian volcano. I turned from that, not paying it much attention but inquiring for water. I was only allowed a gill which only served to arouse my thirst rather than quench it. The Rovers who did not approve of the coldness and who had ten minutes more than we (the scouts), left to go back to the spot where the bus had left us. Rain soon came and continued to fall for about a half an hour. During this time, we sought refuge under our ground sheets and overcoats, devouring a much needed lunch at the same time. The cold soon became unbearable, but we were unable to do anything then as the rain was falling, and all we could do, was to smile and whistle. When the rain stopped, we removed our temporary shelters and photographed the crater and finally ourselves. We watched this marvelous gift to the earth for many minutes and throwing in stones, but to our surprise, none of them reached the bottom, all were sucked into the sides of the volcano by some kind of gravitation that was unknown to us. The volcano was a lovely site and looking across it, our eyes met the sea in the distance. Looking down, we saw an unbelievable volume of Sulphur that we call the crater. As I watched the crater, some supernatural hand took charge of me and some weird voice made me whisper "God has endowed man with gifts greater than he deserves and the greatest of them are those that we obtain free". And with this whisper, a voice, sweet, encouraging and mystic said, "These are no wonders, but the sentiments you give them, the good you bestow upon them and the horror that is withdrawn from them, make them worthy of your praises, your dreams and your poetry".

I was aroused from my dream and the others told me to come; that they were leaving Soufriere and with some vivacious steps we passed through the same sceneries and living over the same sentiments probably for the last time for some or all of us. We collected souvenirs on our way and as some of us were fresher than others, we went ahead and wanted to regain our destination soon, so as to write down notes on that unforgettable journey. As the way back down was slightly sloped to the lower ground, we had to run down and armed with our staves, we were often saved from falling a hundred feet below. I soon rejoined some of the party at the bus and there we awaited the others.

When all were refreshed and ready we drove away again and we were soon reliving the experience of being bumped about as we drove back through the dry river. We made good speed and soon arrived in Georgetown, where we had the 'bus' repaired and where we stopped to enjoy some of the country scenery. When it was ready once more, we got back in and drove straight for Edinboro, arriving there ironically at 7:40 p.m.

We were all tired and put off all *tetes a tetes* until after supper. When we all recounted the day's experience each of us had, that was hard giving and we were near breaking down. Others said it was one of the greatest adventures anybody could undertake. However, we agreed unanimously that Mt. Soufriere was the greatest site that we had ever beheld.

7. The Day That Combermere Fell In (written in 1993)

1993

Of all the unforgettable days at our beloved Combermere, my most unforgettable is the day that Combermere fell in.

It was a bright, sunny day in 1949 and the golden sun was smiling down on Barbados' only mountain – just 1,100 feet really – and also on a former cane field called Weymouth, then the site of Combermere School now celebrating its 300th birthday. (1993)

On this particular day, the young soldiers (I am sorry, I mean Combermerians) had just performed their diurnal morning routine. This consisted of marching in Indian file, form by form, from prep to upper fifth, from classroom to assembly. There the young soldiers (Combermerians) took up their assumed positions under the watchful eyes of prefects, masters and to cap it all Major (Yes Major Noot).

There stood the slim, ever erect Major Noot, Head master of Combermere, at the podium, looking down at the morning's assembly as if he were some Zeus looking down from Mt. Olympus.

In clear, quick, crisp notes the retired British Major and now feared headmaster of Caw'Mere announced the hymn for morning worship. On this unforgettable day, the hymn chosen was the military and appropriate "Onward Christian Soldiers." This hymn appropriately fitted the occasion but gave no hint of things to come.

Lionel (that is Lionel Gittens) was on stage and at the piano, the only mortal that the Major allowed to be on the platform with him. Lionel was in terrific form and banged on the ivories as he never did before and the young soldiers caught on and sung more lustily than ever before, God was in Heaven, Major Noot on his platform and all was well at Combermere and at this morning's assembly.

As the young soldiers (Combermerians) sang, there was a sudden cracking noise. All ears cocked, including the always cocked ears of 'Noot.' The singing continued uninterruptedly but started to sound a little raggedy, as 'fortissimo' quickly plummeted to 'pianissimo.' Suddenly all is not well with the world nor the beloved and historic Alma Mater, (Caw 'Mere).

As the cracking noise escalated into a loud rumbling noise, prefects and masters tried to <u>shoo</u> their little charges. Upset by the sudden cacophony, the Major bellowed in his best stentorian tones: "Quiet, prefects I want you to help maintain quiet."

Bang! Bang!

That was the sound of falling benches.

Bang! Snap! And the assembly floor started to sway and at the same time started to buckle.

"Earthquake" shouted one student.

"Snakes" shouted another.

"Oh Jesus Christ" shouted a third and maybe our only religious student.

And before you could say "gee Don Bred" Lionel made an Olympic jump straight from the piano, through the open window to the courtyard below.

As if taking their cue from the athletic 'Lionel' and the 'Noot', all hell broke loose. Benches started to fall, so too did the young preppies, as it was every man (this was pre co-ed) and boy for himself. Young ones were trampled by the bigger ones as the floor continued to sway and buckle in the middle.

Your writer was a prefect of set 'C' and was put in charge of one of the first forms. Your writer, then tall and skinny and fairly fast, made it to the door before you could say "Jumping Jeosophat."

On the outside, there was pandemonium.

"It is a fire," said one.

"No snakes," said another.

"No, it is an earthquake," said yet another.

These contradictory calls continued to be heard. People were everywhere and panic was printed on the faces of all the boys and masters at Combermere that ill-fated morning.

People from Roebuck St. started pouring in on the grounds. There were shouts of "Call an ambulance," "Call the fire brigade.

"Call an undertaker" shouted one young wit.

After an hour of this pandemonium, Major Noot could be heard saying over a borrowed loud speaker "Go home, go to your homes and don't return until you hear from us. Listen to your Rediffusion," limpedly bellowed the Major now, not as stentorian and less erect than before.

It was fun to see the various masters looking after themselves. Early in the lead were the youthful masters, Muff (Holder), Harry (Sealy), Beasly (Seale) and not to be outdone and close on their heels were the not too youthful ones: The Bull (Williams), Bing (Corbin), Graphie (Pilgrim), and the not too skinny ones like: Perko (Perkins) and Small Cakes (Brooker).

Disaster, like death, is a "Leveller." Young and old, fat and skinny, master and student were all reduced to one crying disheveled mass of humanity.

The ambulances arrived, the injured were rushed to the then General Hospital at Jemmotts Lane. By evening the premises were clear. Only police rescue squads and government officials remained on the premises.

The school was closed for about a month. When it reopened, the juniors were sent to the Garrison under Mr. Lionel Gittens and the seniors remained at Weymouth, but only allowed to use the upper floors.

After the usual government investigation, the committee's findings were not surprising. Then, like now, corruption was responsible.

You see, before Combermere was built, the land was used for planting canes and there was only one big house near the Harrison

17

College end. There lived the late Cameron Hewitt (accountant) and family.

The then government bought the land and cleared it of canes and proceeded to build 'Combermere' without any extra reinforcement or without digging a deep enough foundation. Word also had it that a lot of the material that should have gone into building 'Combermere', instead went into the building of quite a few middle-class homes.

Your writer had many unforgettable days at the 'Mere', but without a doubt, his most unforgettable was the day that Combermere fell in.

(Written by Alfie (Carlton) Gill who later went on to be an assistant master at Combermere and is now an adjunct professor at B.M.CC, the largest of the colleges of the City University of New York.)

8. Humour From The Old Combermere

1993 (FOR 300TH ANNIVERSARY)
Quiz
(See how many of these former students you can identify)

1. **Q.** Who was the student when asked the meaning of the word 'unaware' eagerly answered "Please sir, the last thing my father takes off at night.

    Answer - That heady student later became an assistant master at a secondary school on the West Coast, and hailed from one of the villages in St. Michael close to Government House/

2. **Q.** Who was the boy who when called upon to recite the poem "Oh mistress 'mine' where are you roaming?" jumped up and shouted "Oh mistress 'Minnie' where are you roaming?

    Answer - That student went on to become one of Barbados' top detectives. There was something salty about his name as well.

3. **Q.** Who was the boy from St. George when asked to pronounce the word 'Jeopardy', answered "Please sir, it is gee-oh-par-dee."

    Answer – He too became a policeman and his name is the same as a district in St. George.

4. **Q.** Who was the fifth former when asked the question during religious knowledge always answered "The Jews". Then one day when asked who crucified Jesus, answered, "Please sir, I don't know". From that day on he was stuck with the nickname "Jews".

19

Answer – The fifth former grew up to become – A Barbados Federal and regional civil servant. He always planned to cross a famous river.

5. **Q.** Who was the prefect that when his ham sandwich was taken by some second formers kept in a whole class at lunch and lectured them on the 7th commandment and the importance of the Larceny Act?

   Answer – He grew up to be an economist, an attorney, a journalist and a diplomat.

6. **Q.** Who was the new boy at old Combermere who wore a new blazer for the first day of school? His classmates then tied his blazer into such a small and tight knot, that the more the 'Buff' (Rev. Armstrong) tried to unknot it, the more it tore into shreds.

   Answer – He later became an acting master at Combermere, private school principal, politician for a brief time, writer and college professor.

(This contribution was made by Prof. Alfie (Carlton) Gill who now resides in the U.S.A.) (Attended Combermere 1944-1950)

SECTION II
Education

1. Planning Education for the 21st Century

Recently in June (1994) this writer along with some prestigious educators came to Princeton, New Jersey to dream and to plan for education in the soon-to-be born 21st century.

The conference was sponsored by the N.Y.C. Board of Education which brought eminent educators from some of the most prestigious schools of learning. The site chosen could not have been better. Scanticon is a conference center in New Jersey and is set in the midst of the most breath-taking surroundings in Princeton.

The enchanting buildings were set in the midst of the most verdant pastures and perfumed by some of the most luscious, aromatic flowers. All of this work of nature was watched over by giant species of oak, elm ash and others too numerous to name. As one relished with ecstasy this gorgeous site, one could not help but recall the immortal words of the English poet, John Keats, "A thing of beauty is a joy forever."

This unforgettable conference set records in tackling some of some of the most formidable topics in education. In plenary sessions, conferees heard some of the most earth-shaking proposals for reforming Western education and for the world-wide eradication of illiteracy.

When not in plenary session the conferees met in workshops where the real donkey work was done. There were position papers and heated discussion on a wide range of subjects that included non-traditional methods of teaching, redesigning school buildings, doing away with examinations and replacing both regular and special education with the new cure-for-all, namely "inclusion".

One wished there could have been an educator present from the election-fever island of Barbados who could have recommended the abolition of an archaic notion called the "Common Entrance Examination."

A highlight of the most relevant topic follows.

C. Alfie Gill

PLACES OF FUN

There is a saying in North America, "Learning is fun." It was felt that the Dickensian-looking structures resembled anything except schools.

MULTI-PURPOSE BUILDINGS

Conferees felt that buildings in (1) above should be multi-purpose buildings, housing schools, social centers and government offices such as: unemployment, labor, public assistance and comprehensive health care facilities.

Day care, kindergarten, elementary and junior high schools will be all wings of modern aesthetically designed buildings. Now that more women work, there is a greater need for day care and other childhood centers.

The psychiatrists present felt that the early years were not only the formative years but were the most important in children's lives. It was wittily suggested that since more women could no longer stay home and rear their young ones, then parents (includes fathers) could take their young to work or as near their work places as possible.

Just imagine the benefits to be derived. The more hugging and loving children get, the more secure they feel and become. This restoration of love in children's lives will lead to a reduction in crime and other youthful aberrations. The absent conferee from Barbados would have nodded her agreement.

ADULT LEARNING CENTERS

"People do not stop learning, so why should they stop going to school?" asked one educator.

The second type of multi-purpose structures would house: high schools, colleges, adult learning centers, recreation centers, theaters, museums and art galleries.

Life has become too hectic and complicated. People need to live, work and learn in a simpler, more structured environment.

24

The proximity of all these centers will cut down on tension and travelling, thus freeing up more time for learning, play or just old-time relaxation.

"INCLUSION IS THE WAY TO GO"

All the workshops were equally as deep and serious with position papers by experts who no doubt had put in many years of research.

What obtains in schools in Barbados and most places, Americans call 'regular' education. Students are grouped by ability, hence the bright students are put in 'A' classes and the least bright in classes with letters lower down in the alphabet.

Years ago American schools moved away from this monolithic concept. In its place they introduced mainstreaming and special education.

Mainstreaming classes are mostly regular ed. classes whose students are not in need of special education. Special education was first introduced in 1972 and the federal government mandated special education for children with deficits in learning. These range from mild cases of L.D. (Learning Disabled) to M.R. (mentally retarded) and autistic.

The latest proposal is to do away with both mainstreaming and special education and educate all children in the same atmospheres. This is called "inclusion".

Inclusion is still being debated, but in the areas where it was tried, the results have been phenomenal, especially in Japan.

Maybe in the age of (quasi)-integration, Barbadians need to talk to residents of the twin island state of Trinidad and Tobago. If they did, Barbadians would be reminded that the eleven-plus examination is too nerve racking, too traumatic and injurious to the self-esteem of young children. The eleven-plus helps to perpetuate the class divisiveness and increasing crime and drop-out rate which are threatening return to Barbados to a state of mediocrity.

ABOLISHING EXAMINATIONS

One other workshop that produced a lot of attention was one agitating for the abolition of examinations in schools and colleges.

Barbadians can testify to the unfairness and devastation used to be caused, by the old Senior Cambridge type of examination where a student did not get his/her diploma because he/she failed one subject, such as English or Mathematics.

Instead of the traditional examinations students will have a profile kept on them from day one. There would also be a part of the students' best work as well as evaluations by their teacher and peers.

Educators at the historic Princeton conference argued this recommended method of judging students was superior to the traditional way of passing and failing examinations.

THE COMMON ENTRANCE EXAM

One subject that was not discussed was what Barbadians thought about the "Common Entrance Exam" or the "eleven Plus".

If a conferee from Barbados was here she would have heard the demerits of this anachronistic left over from the antedelical period. All children are not equal, all children do not go to school at the same time; above all children do not learn at the same rate.

With all these uncommon features and inequalities, could you have a meaningful <u>common</u> entrance examination?

No doubt CANA NEWS reported early in July that Trinidad and Tobago had abolished their C.E.E. (Common Entrance Examinations.) Isn't it about time that Barbados did the same?

CONCLUSION

While Barbadians are fiddling in education, the rest of the world will be moving into the 21st century in their multi-purpose buildings, practicing "inclusion" and above all doing away with traditional examinations.

Prof. Carlton (Alfie) Gill lives in New York and teaches at B.M.C.C. C.U.N.Y. He was a former educator in Barbados where he was the principal of Regent High School as well as a former assistant master at Combermere.

2. A Plan To Modify The Out-Of-Seat Behavior of P.W., One Of My Seventh Grade M.I.S.I. Special Education Students.

PART I

P.W. is thirteen years old and is in the seventh grade in the Special Education Unit of J.H.S./275. He is one of a twin. His twin brother is in the eighth grade and is in a regular education class.

P.W. is a tall, slim, light-complexioned youth, who is very likeable. The behavior I selected most in need of modification is his constantly out-of-seat behavior.

BASE LINE

After selecting the behavior most in need of change, I shall discuss the same with the subject of study – P.W.

Then I shall informally observe and record the same. After doing this, I shall start to do a base-line report form on P.W. and also keep a line graph showing his out-of-seat behavior.

The teacher is always hoping for an intrinsic change in the student, but to induce and bring about a permanent change in the student, the teacher must give rewards and use other reinforcements to help bring about a change in the student's negative behavior. One of the techniques in particular which I shall use is the P.P.M. or positive performance model.

THE POSITIVE PERFORMANCE MODEL

The Positive Performance Model (P.P.M.) is one that provides a systematic and analytic approach at developing a behavior change strategy. The P.P.M. I shall use, will seek to implement many of the strategies and skills so ably taught in this course.

This will be supplemented by a base-line buttressed with charts, statistics and varying demographics. The P.P.M. is preferred as it helps us to correctly modify the student's behavior and helps us to customize a plan appropriate to our subject's needs.

PART II
CASE HISTORY OF P.W.

P.W. was born on October 1977. He is one of a twin. His <u>twin</u> brother is in the eighth grade and is in a regular ED. Class and appears well adjusted. My student however (P.W.) has a mild LD (learning disability) and is also a behavioral problem.

P.W.'s mother had four children including P.W. and his twin. Then there is a younger sister and a baby brother (just eighteen months old).

P.W.'s mother seemed to have been overcome by personal problems and could not take care of her family. Her sister, rather than see her niece and twin nephews put in foster homes, volunteered to keep the three older siblings, while the mother kept the baby boy. She also left the East New York area and moved herself and her problems to Coney Island.

When I went to write the annual I.E.P. update on P. W., I went through his Special Education file among the documents I read were (1) P.W.'s case history and (2) it's accompanying psychologist's evaluation report.

P.W. was referred to them by his mother in 1983 because of his lack of academic progress and also because he was held back in the second grade. Interestingly, however is the fact that his twin brother did not experience these difficulties and made all his grades on time. P.W.'s twin brother is now in a regular 8th grade class, whereas P.W. is still trying to mature in a special education MIS I class.

Psychological Testing discovered, "an insecure, anxious, socially aware youngster with intense feelings associated with failure." The test also found he was "Preoccupied with fatherly images and identification."

It appeared that in 1983 P.W. was longing for the image of a father, who was never there and in my layman's point of view, in 1991 he was longing for a mother, who was no longer there. P.W. has very strong and intense feelings on this subject.

He feels his aunt (and now his guardian) favors her children over him and his brother. In addition, he feels that his aunt's husband is too authoritarian and that the uncle-in-law has no right to discipline him and his brother.

I find that because of these inner tensions and feeling of insecurity cause him to perform many anti-social acts and to become a chronic behavior problem. This is a pity, because academically his work has tremendously improved and as a result he was mainstreamed in art and science. During Black History month (February), there was a school-wide daily contest on famous Black Heroes and P.W. swept the board. He took the most top honors and was proclaimed the most outstanding student in Social Studies, a designation that brought honor to his 7 MI Class.

However, in spite of all this P.W. is an enigma. He can go from one extreme (very bad) to the other extreme. He is very argumentative and defiant of authority. He is also very manipulative and tries to get teachers and others to break the school rules in order to try to accommodate him. For example: (1) He tries to get staff to buy sodas from the teachers' cafeteria for him or (2) He will misstate his age on working papers. Saying 'no' to these requests leads to inappropriate behavior from him. He is constantly out of his seat, talks without permission or raising his arm, in addition, he is always eating.

After reviewing all the above with him, the behavior we selected for modification was his "Out-of-seat behavior." (See attachments)

AFTER THE PRE-PLANNING STAGE

I met with the subject of this plan and discussed with him the existence of certain negative behavior traits and his willingness to change.

After much discussion and prioritizing of behavior traits, we both agreed that the trait most in need of change was his out-of-seat behavior.

One Friday in late February, I met with P.W. I congratulated him on being a good student, told him his grades were good, but that I thought that there was one area in which he could improve. I opened with an open-ended question and closed with a closed-ended question to which he gave an affirmative statement 'yes,' he would like to stay in his seat more. In this conversation, I used both re-enforcers, e.g. smiles and praise. I also used empathy, statements to win him. I used positive phrasing to let him know that his feelings were understood and accepted. He then posed this open-ended question: "What can I do to stay in my seat more?"

I promised to augment this with material rewards, namely an ice-cream for the first full day of in-seat behavior and a certificate at the end of the first full week. I then drew up a contract between us and we both signed. (See enclosures)

P.W.'s work and conduct conform to the definition of "learning Disables" found in PL 94-142, which says INTER alia "all Learning Disability (LD) Students have an academic problem in one or more areas due not to emotional disturbance, etc."

P.W. is definitely having problems in achieving due to his hyperactivity, his constant talking and constant out-of-seat behavior. P.W. has very strong and intense feelings for one his age. He also seems compelled to act these out in class. To quote Dr. Haim G. Ginott who wrote in his famous work "Between Parent and Child". (Ginott, Haim, G. 1965)

"All feelings are legitimate, the positive, the negative and the ambivalent."

This sentiment is also shared by Siegel E. and Smith J.E., in *"Educating the Learning Disabled"* (1986).

To help modify P.W.'s behavior and increase his in-seat behavior, I first resorted to pre-planning. I also drew up charts showing the number of times P.W. was out of his seat. (See enclosures) I read a number of works to assist me including Charles, C.M. 1985 – Classroom Discipline (P.P.M.)

I followed this up with a Positive Performance Model mentioned earlier. Some of the strategies I decided to use included: rewards, positive phrasing, the empathy statement, supporting and approval statements, sometimes dispersed with humor and other non-confrontational strategies. The style of teaching I use, in particular with P.W., is called clinical teaching.

In clinical teaching, the teacher is somewhat of a "child watcher". With P.W. my goal was to tailor learning experiences to P.W.'s particular and unique needs. This is a style of teaching recommended by Norris, Harding, McCormick, Linda (1990). "Exceptional Children and Youth"

BEHAVIORAL OBJECTIVE

Goals and objectives are the methods by which the limits of acceptable behavior are set. In P.W.'s case, the objective was that during a 40 minute class-room period, P.W. will increase the duration of IN-SEAT BEHAVIOR from 10 minutes to 15 minutes, for one week. This parameter had to be changed a few times before arriving at a practical time limit.

POSITIVE PERFORMANCE MODEL

This is based on the dictum, that the more frequently a behavior is rewarded, the greater the probability that it would persist. To help induce and increase P.W.'s In-Seat-Behavior, I had to reward him ranging from praise to his favorite ice-cream. After three weeks, I was able to increase his In-Seat Behavior by almost 100%. (See enclosures)

SUPPORTING/EMPATHY STATEMENTS

To help bring about this increase in his In-Seat Behavior, I had to practice skills such as positive phrasing and using the empathy statement. I used the empathy statement to help get P.W. to refocus his attention and to point to our success. In increasing his In-Seat Behavior. In the beginning, it had to be coupled with material rewards, but later, praise alone sufficed. P.W. by no way is a perfect student academically and behaviorally.

On April 16, P.W. never left his seat, something no other student had achieved. I rewarded him with an ice-cream and told him what a wonderful student he was. I then promised to reward him weekly rather than daily with material rewards. At first he was very reluctant to settle for non-material rewards, but now he does and without complaining. In the Post-Modification Period, results show the following: In the first Post-Mod week, his In-Seat Behavior increased 75% in one week. In one week, it declined a little to 70% and in one week it shot back up to 80%, which is where it is right now. I am very excited about this improvement.

This change is due mainly to the agreement and motivation I received from our able and dedicated Professor, Victor Tasio as well as from my fellow students. I also derived encouragements from the writings of Fraiberg, S.H. (1959) and Ginott, H.G. (1965) mentioned earlier.

BIBLIOGRAPHY

1. Charles, C.M. (1985). "Building a class-room"
2. Fraiberg, S.H. (1959). "The magic years"
3. Ginott, H. G. (1965. "Between parent and child"
4. Norris, Harding: Mccormick, Linda (1990). "Exceptional children and youth"
5. Public Law 94-142. Special education
6. Siegal, E. AND Gold R. (1982). "Educating the learning disabled"

3. The Founding Of The Democratic Labour Party

It has been incorrectly stated that the Democratic Labour Party (DLP) was formed at Land's End, Westbury Road. This misstatement is what historians would characterize as a piece of revisionism. The DLP was formed at the Regent High School, then at Roebuck Street (next to Linton's Garage). The principal of the Regent High School was (Carlton) Alfie Gill, who was the first assistant secretary of the party. All the acts of formation took place at Roebuck Street, no matter what the revisionists write. It was also there that the nomination of the late Edwin Zephirin and Sir Douglas Lynch were put on hold due to the principal objections of Professor Gill, Owen T. Allder and L.B. Brathwaite. All this could be verified by checking with distinguished founding members like Sir Fedrick Smith and Mr. Pasty Springer. A party is formed where it is factually formed, no matter what revisionists write.

PS: Sir Frederick Smith and the Hon. J. Patsy Springer both passed away in 2016.

The Regent High School was a private Secondary School founded by Alfie Gill in 1952 at the tender age of 23. Like the other private secondary schools, they no longer exist. The school is remembered by its former students through the Regent High Schools Old Scholar's Association Chapters which are still in existence in London, Canada, USA and Barbados.

(Letter to the Nation Newspaper)

4. Exceptional Children

(Including the Disabled)

PROJECT ONE

The book chosen for this paper is entitled "Exceptional Children and Youth" and ably written by Norris Haring and Linda McCormick. These are among the leading experts in the field of special education.

A catalyst for in special education was the civil rights movement which culminated in the 1954 U.S. Supreme Court decision in <u>Brown v Board of Education</u> (Topeka). This case ruled once and for all that the doctrine of separate but equal inherently wrong. This decision affirmed education is a right of all Americans including those with learning disabilities.

A legislative landmark was reached on Nov. 29, 1975 when public law 94-142 was passed. This law mandated that for a school system to receive public funds, it must provide for a free, public education for every child between the ages of 3 and 21, regardless of how seriously such a child may be handicapped. This is based on the premise that all children can benefit from an education. This includes the services that go with such right including: - transportation, counselling and speech therapy.

The authors emphasize that all children receiving special education and related services should be fairly and accurately evaluated. The authors further pointed out that a handicapped student's education must be appropriate to such child's individual capacities and needs. This is a requirement of PL 94-142.

For each child or youngster receiving public assistance, the authorities must develop an I.E.P. (individual educational plan). The I.E.P. must be prepared annually and must include statements on the child's present level of functioning, long-term educational goals and short-term measurable objectives.

These goals must be realistic and should honestly show where the youth is at. The more honest and realistic an I.E.P. is, the more effective it becomes. The student's work and behavior must be carefully monitored and from the requisite feed-back; the I.E.P should be updated to reflect an show the mastery of any of the set goals.

The authors also argue that handicapped children and youth must be educated in the least restrictive atmosphere possible. A student should not be placed in a more restrictive setting than is necessary or except the gains from such placement exceed the liabilities. It must not be forgotten that the ultimate goal is the mainstreaming of the student.

PL-94-142 states that all LD (learning disabled students) have an academic problem in one or more areas and are not achieving in accordance with their potential ability. Learning disabilities have been put in four categories: - acquired trauma, genetic/hereditary influences, bio-chemical abnormalities and environmental influences. Some LD students show characteristics in more than one. In my M.I.S. I 7th grade class right now I have students who have characteristics in more than one area. For example, some may show genetic influences as well as environmental influences.

There is a variety of methods for teaching the learning disabled. The five (5) foremast teaching methods are: language programs; multi-sensory approaches; data-based instruction, (DBI); direct instruction and cognitive behavior modification. In addition to these, mainstreaming is the next frequently used tool. Very often as teachers, we find ourselves resorting to one or more of these remedies.

A behavior that is most common to my students and which I always try to modify is that, of out-of-seat behavior. To help modify this behavior, I first meet with the student and together we meet and identify the behavior to be modified. The student then enters a written contract with the teacher and class. Some of the techniques I use with my students to modify their behavior are: rewards, positive phrasing, the empathy statements. This form of teaching is known as clinical teaching and is highly recommended by Haring and McCormick in their highly-publicized book.

I also read "Between Parent and Child" by Dr. Haim G. Ginott (1965) and as both parent and teacher, I find Ginott's approach refreshing and practical. One of my favorite quotations from Ginott is as follows: "All feelings are legitimate, the positive, the negative and the ambivalent."

If as teachers we will remember this, we can have a more rewarding time with our LD (learning disabled) students.

5. The Benefits Of Cooperative Education

INTRODUCTION

What is Co-Operative education?

Co-operative Education is a set of practical strategies which any teacher may employ to promote increased learning and better social skills. It is said that in unity, there is strength and as teachers we must always be on the alert and maximize the learning opportunities for our students.

One of the tools for enhancing and increasing our students' learning is that of co-operative learning. Traditional classroom practice is oriented toward individualistic and competitive learning. CL (co-operative learning), is therefore a new boy on the block and as a result, sometimes meets with resistance from the old timers who are steeped in the traditional methods.

What are some of the advantages of co-operative learning with the students in the regular classes? Co-operative learning methods lead to phenomenal results. The main-stream students become better motivated but above all they learn to share and to help other members of their group. This interdependence helps teachers a lot.

Instead of all the weight being on the teacher, the brighter students help the slower ones, but eventually everyone benefits. The students behave better and the brighter students help the slower ones by communicating with each other in language they are accustomed to using.

It is a joy to go in a classroom and see the students engrossed in their work and busily and cooperatively helping each other.

About a year ago, a colleague told me about Co-operative Learning and I then vowed to learn more about it. That is why I am taking this particular course being ably taught by the present Professor. By learning how to establish heterogeneous co-operative groups, teachers can transform the academic achievements of their students and boost the morale of their schools.

Class Profile

I am an eighth (8) grade Special Education Teacher in a Junior High School situated in the poorer section of Brooklyn, N.Y. My class is a M.I.S. 1, that is my students are slightly learning disabled and their I.E.P.'s (individual learning plans) are aimed at M.I.S.1 goals.

M.I.S. to the uninitiated stand for modified instruction services, and M.I.S. 1 means that the students in a M.I.S. 1 class are the least difficult and can function with a teacher alone, on the other hand, the students an a M.I.S. 2 class are more severely handicapped and call for a para-professional to be in the classroom as well.

There are thirteen students in my class; ten boys and three girls. Their ages range from 13 to 15. They have all applied to high schools for admission and at least ten of them are sure to be admitted.

Last year I taught a M.I.S. 1 7th grade class, whose members were at times a little hyper, but who always did their class work and home-work. This year, I was given a class of low-functioning eighth grade. They are chronic cutters, persistent behavioral problems and above all have an aversion to doing any kind of class-work or home-work.

The first half of the present semester I used traditional teaching techniques, since I felt I had not yet acquired enough teaching techniques in co-operative learning and I was almost burnt out from the daily fights with my M.I.S. 1 class. It was a constant battle. I had to fight to get them to both (1) work and (2) behave.

Last October I enrolled in a current class in Co-operative Education sponsored by school District 23, in Brooklyn, and put on by and ably taught by Professor Barbara Ellis.

Trying Co-operative Learning In The Class-Room

After school returned from Christmas recess I decided to try Co-operative learning in my class-room. I divided the class into four (4) cooperative learning groups. There are three groups with three students each and one with four students,

This is one of the greatest moves I ever made as a teacher. The students quickly got into the co-operative spirit and were soon busily helping each other. The better working ones went around helping the slower ones.

I started competition within the groups to see who was the best of the group. I simultaneously started a weekly competition between the Groups and by the stroke of a pen (co-operative learning) worked, I almost solved my problem. Class 8D2 greatly improved in work and conduct. This improvement has been noticed by both my supervisor and the principal and the parents of my students.

Now I am more relaxed and no longer nearly burned out. A number of books including two by Johnson and Johnson. I also studied other authors including (1) Jacob Kounin and (2) Haim Ginott (one of my favorite authors).

Individual Profiles

I have selected for in –depth study and for behavior modification strategies two of my students (a) K.W. and (b) A.J.

1. Student K.W. – Biography

K.W. is a young male age fourteen (14), and comes from a family of four (4) including two (2) older brothers and a sister, aged nine (9). K.W. is from a one-parent home and lives with his mother and other siblings. K.W. has a lot of anger and hostility in him. He is very suspicious of and resentful to strangers or people new to him. He used to curse constantly and used more obscene than clean words.

Pre – Cooperative Education Period

AS far as work is concerned, he is very lazy. He begins tasks but never finishes them. Very often, all he has on the note paper is his name, date and subject. Sometimes, with a little luck, he got as far as writing the aim of the particular subject. For the first half of the semester he scored all 55's except in GYM. It should be noted that 55 is a failing grade.

Post – Cooperative Education Period

I discussed K.W.'s work and conduct with all his subject teachers, his guidance counselors, as well as my supervisor and his mother. We discussed different strategies to get K.W. to improve in his work and conduct. He then wrote a number of contracts which we both signed. In each, he agreed to refrain from doing negative things and to improve in his behavior and work habits.

To help him achieve these, I gave him a variety of awards ranging from a cartoon watch to class certificates. I am proud to say that since resorting to these measures, his work and conduct have greatly improved. However, a lot of his improvement is due to the introduction of co-operative learning techniques.

Because of co-operative learning, he was able to receive personalized, individual help from members of his group. As a result, his grades have improved and so also has his self –esteem. Not only will I thank Johnson and Johnson for Co-operative Learning and the success it brought, I can also praise my 8th grade Class.

(II) Student A.J. – Biography

Profile: A.J. is a fourteen-year-old female. She is in the 8th grade and is in my M.I.S. 1 Eighth Grade Class. She lives with her unwed mother and ten (10) brothers and sisters.

Pre-Co-op Period

A.J.'s I.E.P. shows she is severely learning disabled and on the border line between M.I.S. I and M.I.S. II. In her last class, she was described as being one of the class low-functioning students. Her forte was cutting classes and finding excuses not to attend class.

I spoke to her, her teachers, parents and counsellors. Then I had her draw up contracts to modify her work habits and conduct.

I put her in a co-operative group with understanding students, and did it work?

Post-Co-Op Period

She accepted the challenge and decided on her own to change (with the encouragement of her teachers and group members of course).

A.J. is now reading better because of the help given to her by her Group Members. Now that her grades have improved, she is coming to class more and doing more of her work. Her enhanced grades have also led to greater self-esteem.

EVALUATION

Co-operation is as old as mankind, but co-operative learning as a tool of learning is fairly new. Thanks to Johnson and Johnson, more and more is being written on the subject.

Co-operation between Group Members is a prerequisite to success. This in turn leads to competition between groups. This competition leads to greater learning since co-operation and not competition is the desired result. The teacher must control any over-competitiveness and accentuate the positive, namely co-operative learning.

Meetings between all parties involved with the students is another tool in the co-operative learning repertoire; to quote an old saying 'anything that one does, two could do better'.

The atmosphere In the class room must promote the co-operative learning style and de-emphasize selfishness and over competitiveness. This also leads to better social skills.

CONCLUSION

Co-operative learning is a good tool and like everything else, it requires practice. After some practice, teachers will find that the more they use it, the better they become at it.

To quote directly from Johnson and Johnson, "Students who have had extensive co-operative learning experiences have been found to have more and small group skills than did students who have primarily experienced competitive and individualistic experiences". (Johnson & R. Johnson – 1983)

Co-operative learning is here to stay. Now let more teachers make greater use of it. Not only academically but in the area of social skills and human relations, our students become better persons. Better friends and better human beings will they be.

Thanks to Co-operative Learning.

6. Churches' HIV Message Clear

As loud as the message is that condoms can protect against HIV, the message of abstinence, faithfulness and monogamy will be shouted even more loudly.

This is the position churches across Barbados, particularly those under the umbrella of the Barbados Evangelical Association (BEA), will be taking.

They will also be sending the message: "Know your HIV status", and will be urging members of their congregations to cast aside any fears they had and get tested.

These comments were made during the question-and-answer session after a lecture delivered by Professor Alfie Gill yesterday morning at the Bethel Evangelical Church, Grazettes, St Michael.

General Secretary and Chief Executive Officer of the Evangelical Association of the Caribbean, Reverend Gerry Seale, said he was concerned that there seemed to be a division in the messages about HIV/AIDS.

He said the church was saying abstinence, faithfulness and monogamy, and the Government "condomise". What he would really like to see was both groups working together rather than "shooting at each other".

Seale added that the much talked-about distribution of condoms in prison was a "red herring". "emotive" and "irrelevant"; neither did he see how legalizing prostitution would stop people from getting AIDS or another disease.

President of the BEA, Reverend Dr. Nigel Taylor agreed with Gill who said the church had a greater role to play in the fight against the AIDS pandemic.

Taylor added that HIV/AIDS was not a church or young people issue, but a societal one that would impact on the lives of those in the 20 to 25 age group and in the 40s, the productive sector.

In his lecture, which looked at the HIV/AIDS on Blacks, Gill said the disease was having a serious impact on those women over 50 in Brooklyn, United States. He also called for the church to set the example and not discriminate or blame people for their HIV status.

By Prof. C. Alfie Gill
(Member of U.N. AIDS Committee)

45

7. HIV Less Likely Among Circumcised

There appears to be a link between more uncircumcised males contracting HIV than those who are circumcised.

That's according to a visiting professor, Carlton Gill.

Gill's assertion came as he handed over items to the National HIV AIDS Commission to help with the current sensitization program.

"It is an issue that is being overlooked here in Barbados and I strongly believe that if we don't pay closer attention to this link, the outcome will be unpleasant." He said.

Professor Gill referred to a recent study conducted by the World Health Organization (WHO) that stated that there was compelling evidence that male circumcision reduced the risk of heterosexually-acquired HIV infection in men by approximately 60 per cent.

"Barbadian males who were not circumcised as infants should not be afraid to have the procedure done now they are adults. It could possibly save their lives by reducing the chances of contracting HIV," he said.

The WHO study also concluded that the male circumcision provided only partial protection and therefore should be only one element of a comprehensive package that included the provision of HIV testing and counselling services; treatment of sexually transmitted infections; the promotion of safer sex practices; and the provision of male and female condoms and the promotion of their correct and consistent use.

Lecture given on January 10, 2010 in N.Y.

Printed in the Nation – Sunday Sun Jan.

8. HIV/AIDS in Barbados

Lecture August 2004

Distinguished ladies and gentlemen, brothers and sisters:

Greetings from New York especially the N.Y.C. Coalition of Faith Based Organizations. The coalition consists of many churches, mosques and some synagogues. It's headed by two chairpersons; one male and one female. In 2003 Sister Anita Parker, M.S.W. (a Jamaican) and yours truly were elected as co-chairpersons and in June (two months ago), we put on our second annual forum on H.I.V./A.I.D.S., entitled "Struggling with the Spirits".

Believe me Brothers and Sisters, it is a struggle to rescue and preserve Homo Sapiens and there is even a greater struggle going on to save the Negroid race which is being heavily decimated by this pandemic even as we speak. Last July I was invited to the 8th annual conference on "Sexuality and A.I.D.S." at the prestigious School of Divinity (at Howard University) in the nation's capital. The title of their conference was "Breaking the Silence".

Yes, Brother and Sisters, we must break the silence because if we don't, our race, (the Negroid race) will be wiped out before our very eyes. This is no mere exaggeration on my part or crying wolf. Brothers and Sisters, the wolf is here devouring the best and youngest and recently it has started to devour our seniors as well. The fastest growing segment in New York City is among the 50 plus age group. Yes, this is surprising but this is happening as we sit here. I shall quote a lot of statistics, but behind every statistic, there is a human face. The face of a parent, even a grandparent, a husband, sister, cousin, husband, wife, lover or friend.

Yes! Speechifying or being judgmental will not save lives; it is too late for that. For those who have already contracted the virus, it is time for T.L.C. (Tender Loving Care), compassion, affordable drugs and the prayers of our respective religious or non-religious organizations. Whether it is a mutation of an earlier virus, a sudden and brand new virus, or as may be the case, it could be a man-made laboratory-hatched disease; such is the genius and evil of man. It must be remembered that during the second world war in the United States of America in the state of Alabama, two hundred Afro-American males suffering from S.T.D.s were left untreated, so the experimental scientists could conduct what became known as the "Tuskegee Experiment". So much for love of their fellow-man. Do you remember the words of Longfellow? "Tell me not in mournful numbers, life is but an empty dream".

The first-known cases of A.I.D.S. were recorded about thirty years ago. In those years, it was decimating mainly Caucasian males. Very few persons of African extraction were dying from it, except the rare entertainer and/or clothes designer. The real powers of this world, the rich, mighty and powerful, discussed among themselves at Lodges, Synagogues or Halls of Power, and said, this A.I.D.S. thing would be a good thing to introduce into their community of color. Negroids are often referred to as "they" and "them".

Do you remember the Malthusian theory? That one way to hold down the world's population was to carry out a few wars. So we had World Wars I and II and countless mini wars, but the effect was to vastly reduce the number of Caucasoids, which meant that the Black, Brown and yellow peoples of the earth would soon take over. Remember the number 666? Well Caucasoids did in this speaker's opinion. It was accidentally, even intentionally introduced into the Black and Brown communities, where today H.I.V/ A.I.D.S. is devastating whole populations. Don't forget about the Tuskegee Experiment.

Now for some cold, hard statistics. Don't cringe in your seats but resolve to respond with love and to help combat this decimator of the earth's population. First to refresh your memory, H.I.V. is the virus that causes A.I.D.S. With H.I.V., the body's cells lose the ability to fight off illness. Note: there are varying periods that it takes H.I.V. to progress into A.I.D.S. but in most of the studied cases, it took about ten years. How is H.I.V. passed on? The most common ways are through unprotected sex, by sharing needles or injection equipment, tainted blood from a blood transfusion and most touchingly from mother to child. These are the known causes.

In 2002, there were more than 42 million reported cases world-wide. In the United States of America there are over one million reported cases of H.I.V. and in Sub-Sahara Africa there were 29 million and only 4 million of them are getting treatment. Why oh why? In New York City where I live it is estimated that about 16% òf the population is H.I.V. positive. It is said that one in every seven Black males is positive. I don't know the exact statistics for Barbados, but let us assume it is one in twenty. Do you know what that means? That 5% of the people in this room would test positive. Frightening but true. Now let us turn our sights on the continent of Africa. Here, the story is more heart-breaking and the figures more depressing. In Africa there are more than 30 million known cases and you can multiply that number by two for a more realistic figure.

Frightening but true, in some African countries the figures are terribly depressing, especially in the countries of Uganda, Lesotho and South Africa. In Lesotho it is estimated that over 30% of the population test positive and with no cure in sight. (Why oh why?) South Africa has 5 million cases. Now let us come to our part of the world, namely the Caribbean. In Jamaica there are over 30 new cases a week and over twelve deaths a week. Trinidad has close to 30 new cases a week and 8 to 10 deaths.

Now, Barbados, it is estimated has 2 cases a day or over 700 new cases a year and over 200 deaths. Mind you, I am using conservative estimates not to alarm and scare you even more. Brothers and Sisters, as death is no respecter of persons so is H.I.V./A.I.D.S. It affects all types and conditions of people: rich and poor, young and old, Black and White, straight and not. This is a pandemic scourge which is reducing populations and rendering poor countries even poorer. Fellow Barbadians, we cannot afford to be complacent. The tentacles of A.I.D.S. are equal and everywhere. The A.I.D.S. victims in Barbados come not only from Gaps and the Village but also from your Heights and Terraces.

As Wordsworth put it "Scepter and Crown must tumble down and in the dust be equal made with poor the crooked scythe and spade". To older folks who think it wouldn't happen to them, let me read you the story of one middle-aged, middle-class Afro-American woman.

READ

If that didn't bring tears to your eyes, nothing will. Well, there are not all bad news. There are a few silver linings as well. First, Uganda which had the highest incidence has some good news. At the world-wide forum recently held in Bangkok, it was reported that the situation in Uganda had stabilized and fewer cases were being reported. It is said that this decline is due to the massive appeal to practice abstinence and a positive response was given by the populace of Uganda.

Next is the story from Thailand. First there was a decline then the population became complacent, practiced safe sex less and guess what? The virus is on the increase again. The lesson from that is that "one swallow does not a summer make". When translated, it means a reduction in numbers is not whipping this epidemic. Let me say emphatically, there is no known cure and none in sight. Whatever medication they have, (anti-retroviral) cost an arm and a leg and will bankrupt most small countries.

I proudly report that one of our coalition members, a young, Oxford-educated Bahamian lawyer is assembling a team of Pro Bono lawyers to negotiate with the pharmaceuticals to get a substantial reduction in the price of drugs. We also have a group of concerned Jamaicans doing the ground work for putting on a conference there (Jamaica) next year, while I dream of a group of Barbadians who will do the same. My coalition will provide literature, speakers and condoms.

So to wrap it up: this pandemic increases exponentially. If you get twelve new cases, there are six new deaths. For those who already have the virus, it may be too late but if we act promptly and decisively, we can limit the number of new cases. In fact, dating in the United States of America, now has some new features. Right away, she wants to know if you were tested and suggest that both of you get tested and guess what? She will be asking you to get retested. This is not Russian roulette, Brothers and Sisters. It is better to be safe than sorry, so my parting words are:

1. Develop and carry out a massive educational program
2. Stress ABSTINENCE. Be sincere, but realistic in doing so
3. It is said "an ounce of prevention is better than a pound of cure"

So that means, males use condoms and you sisters you can use the safest and most reliable forms of female contraceptives.

Brothers and Sisters (Thanks to Longfellow)
"Life is real, Life is Earnest
And the Grave is not its Goal
But to live that each tomorrow
Finds us far better than today".

I thank you.

Speech given August 2004
Bridgetown, Barbados.

Prof. C. Alfie Gill
April 22, 1992

9. Black Civilization Day Celebrated in Barbados

January 6, 2003

Members of the African Diaspora celebrate all kinds of holidays such as Halloween and Guy Fawkes' day. How much more uplifting it is to celebrate a day set aside to recall our African heritage and to thank God and for some, Allah or Jah, for all the accomplishments of the African race and to celebrate the contributions to mankind by people of color.

In particular, we shall like to thank Secretary Kofi Annan and the United Nations for having the wisdom and foresight in designing such a day and Barbados owes a profound gratitude to God for so graciously hosting this lecture and your humble servant graciously thank him for so kindly inviting me to address you here today.

My remarks will be on 'Black civilization and what it means to me.'

All historians and scholars will agree on one thing and that is, there is only one race, the human race, better known as Homo sapiens.

The World Book Britannica and other encyclopedias will tell you that the human race got fragmented and what emerged, we call a sub-species.

The three major sub-species are (1) the Negroid, (2) Caucasoid and (3) the Mongoloid better known as the black, white and yellow races. The word 'races' refers to the afore-mentioned sub-species. I shall remind you often there is only one race that counts and that is the human race.

All life started in Africa and eventually spread throughout the world, commonly known as the planet earth. I refer to one of the earliest works on this subject pre-historic people or the first humans. (See J.A. Rogers, Hadrian etc).

The equator as you all know, passes through Africa and is the hottest part of the earth. That is where life began and that is where Blacks started. After a great continental drift when continents became separate, some of the first humans moved northwards where it is extremely cold and we are talking centuries before central heating was invented.

These northward-bound migrants lived in caves, where for several months of the year, they did not see the sun nor feel its heat. Hence the emergence of the sub-species, we later called Caucasoid.

Caucasoids, I like to think of as Negroids who have lost their dark complexion and healthy curly hair. The Mongoloids later appeared, and as you can guess is really a cross between Black and White. Yellow became the color of this third sub-species and consists mainly of people we refer to as Asiatics.

You were indeed lucky last year to hear firsthand from the renowned scholar and Egyptologist, Dr. Ben. Again we thank you for bringing all this enlightenment to Barbadians, in particular to those I affectionately call Afro-Barbadians.

I am an unapologetic and avowed Christian and therefore accept the biblical explanation of the origin of man.

I refer you to Genesis Chapter 2, according to this, God made man from dust and the last time I saw dust, it was black or brown. This supports the theory that the first people were Negroid. Adam was a Black man, I therefore put it to you that the first woman, Eve, was a black woman. There are two other famous explanations for the origin of man and both support the common ancestry theory.

The first of these two doctrines is Darwin's 'The Origin of the Species' which in no way rebuts the biblical account of the origin of man. One can therefore be a Christian and an evolutionist and this is not an oxymoron.

The third explanation of the origin of Homo sapiens is known as the clinical approach. This approach supports the common ancestor doctrine. Scientific research and experiments have established that people, regardless of their skin color, have a common DNA trait. Likewise there is a commonality in blood types. The best known blood group system is called the ABO with O being the overwhelming blood type. Caucasians also have type O, not a W.

Brothers and Sisters, the other races spend time trying to prove their existence. The only race that does not have this problem, is the world's oldest and most survivor-prone, namely the Negroid race. Because of the fear of extinction, Caucasians developed over-aggressive habits resulting in numerous wars, in particular, World War I and II, or what some scholars refer to as tribal wars.

Now how does all this affect the African and his place in history? The Black man, who was the first man gave to the world the first gifts of knowledge and achievement and left indelible marks of the African history. I refer you to the Pyramids of Egypt, the Sphinx of Alexandria, the Hanging Gardens of Babylon and so on and so on. The Negroid race was the race that gave to the universe, the sciences, art, literature, architecture and mathematics. The first person to count from one to ten was a man of color, a Nubian man – like you.

"Rise up you mighty people" to quote the late Marcus Garvey, great you were and great you will be again. The period known as slavery was but a short interruption in our march of success and accomplishment. Slavery is no shame or disgrace. Nearly all peoples have been enslaved at one time or another. When pope Gregory visited Great Britain, he saw young Angles for sale and likened them to angels. The Jewish people have been enslaved time and time again; first by the Egyptians, later by the Babylonians etc. I refer you to the Old Testament in God's holy book, the Bible.

Just as today's Jews say "never again", all you members of the African Diaspora must say the same "never again". The book of Revelations predicts the end time of the world as we know it, but before it happens, the present rulers, (remnants of the Caucasoid race), will lose their power and the black, brown and yellow people would come into their own.

The race of mighty people referred to by Garvey will rise again. A race that started with Adam and Eve and include: Moses, King David, Solomon (wisest man). Ramases, King Tut and include famous women such as Cleopatra of the Nile, Queen Nefertiti, Charlotte

Amalie, wife of George III and Empress Josephine, wife of Napoleon Bonaparte.

Every time you count from one to ten you must think of Euclid and the first mathematicians. If you climb Mount Everest, the person of color got there first the Sherpa Tenzing Norgay. You can be sure Sir Hillary would have sent him just in case. If you go to the North Pole, again the Afros were there in the person of Matthew Hensen, the Afro-American explorer. While Columbus did not discover any place since he was lost, actually Columbus was <u>discovered</u> lost and forlorn and rescued by the natives of the island of Hispaniola. When the Afro peoples of the world come into their own again, children would again learn genuine history, not what we call that His Story. Caucasian history started in 1942 but black history started with Adam and Eve.

Rise up mighty people, rise up. Great you were before and great you will be again.

I shall like to quote you an excerpt from the monthly Moravian dated November 1986. The Moravian is the name of a monthly magazine that goes into the home of every North American Moravian. The caption, "To be a Christian is to be color-blind" and written by yours truly.

Excerpt

There the writer debunked the myth that the Caucasoids were the superior race. Now to come a little closer to our time, many of the areas of endeavor formerly dominated by Eurocrats have now been mastered and taken over by non-Caucasian people of the earth.

If we look at entertainment the following great names will spring to mind: Paul Robeson, Louis Armstrong, Harry Belafonte, Bob Marley, the Mighty Sparrow, Sidney Poitier and Denzel Washington.

On the female side we have Shirley Bassey, Eartha Kitt, Ella Fitzgerald, Leontyne Price and the foremost opera singer Marian Anderson and Halle Berry.

Now let's turn to the world of sports. If I say cricket, you will immediately name the greats: Sir Frank Worrell, Sir Garfield Sobers,

Sir Vivian Richards, Sir Everton Weekes, the incomparable Brian Lara and our own Wes Hall.

If we go to a sport called baseball, the same thing happens. You will hear names like Jackie Robinson, Hank Aaron, Willie Mays, Reggie Jackson etc.

I shall just like to name two other sports in which it was thought that Afros could not excel, namely tennis and golf. The late Althea Gibson, Arthur Ashe and now the reigning monarchs, the mature, race-conscious, invincible Williams sisters, Serena and Venus, give lie to this.

Next let's turn to golf where it is thought that only Caucasoids would do well (because of their money I suppose.) That myth too was debunked by a together, young Afro-Asian by the name of Tiger Woods. Wake up and rise ye mighty race.

Now let us turn to outstanding world leaders who have mastered the art of peace not only of war. The world owes a lot to: Frederick Douglas, Ralph Bunche, Dr. Martin Luther King, Jr, Malcolm X, and Jesse Jackson of the U.S.A. From Africa we can name such mighty leaders as: Kwame Nkrumah, Jomo Kenyatta, poet, scholar and late president of Guinea, the great Sekou Toure and the names would not be complete without mentioning Nelson and Winnie Mandela and the constantly-under-fire Robert Mugabe of Zimbabwe. And now to come to our little part of this vast universe, we have Desalines and Toussaint (liberators of Haiti), from Jamaica we have Garvey, Bogle, Michael Manley and Nanny of Nannytown. From Trinidad: Uriah Butler, Captain Cipriani, historian and economist, Eric Williams. From the tiny island of Grenada, the great Maurice Bishop, who was snatched away too soon and from our own island in the sun we have Shirley Chisolm, Samuel Jackman Prescod, Charles Duncan O'Neal and Errol Walton Barrow.

Before I conclude I shall like to address some words to the young people of Barbados. I grieve for you daily, I pray for you, I even fast for you.

Excerpt

You are descendants of Kings and Queens, inventors and explorers. Why would you let down this great heritage by copying the degrading, negative and decadent attributes of up north. The behavior, dress and antics that you imitate are not from the literate, cultured Afro-American group, but from a small, socially and economically deprived, under-class or sub-group. Some of the behaviors you imitate were born in prison and allowed to exist for the racist purpose of stigmatizing, depriving and subjugating Afro-American youths. The rulers there know, by not curbing these behaviors, they always will get the good jobs and the prison industry will continue to thrive.

This unacceptable way of dress, i.e. not wearing a belt and letting the crotch of your pants to fall to your knees. Do you know this style came straight out of the jails? In the U.S.A., unlike here, when you go to jail, they take away your belt and shoe laces, hence when the young prisoners are playing basketball, one hand is holding up the pants and the other shooting ball. Young Barbadians, increase your self-esteem, imitate your great African ancestors. If you do, I guarantee crime will go down and this island will again be a paradise.

Recitations

The poorest Caucasoid feels superior to the other races. Why? Because he identifies with the dominant Caucasian race. The surest way to uplift the Black Man is to let young Blacks think of belonging to a great race that once dominated the world and will again.

I bet that when history has forgotten the feats of: Stalin, Hitler and Mussolini, people will still be holding in high regard your fore-bearers in the persons of: Adam, Moses, Jesus, Mohammed, Mahatma Ghandi and Paul Robeson.

God has been good to me and I shall like to testify that the best way to help yourself is to help a fallen brother or sister or some youth in need of guidance and role models. I find that the more we help others, the more God blesses us. I appeal to the "haves" to give something back to your community.

In the U.S.A., on Saturdays, I tutor poor kids in Harlem in reading and math. I have done fairly well in real estate, so I recently started an organization called Y.U.E. – Young Urban Entrepreneurs, teaching young entrepreneurs how to get into real estate and do well at it. I even have my first adherent down here, a young businessman who practices some of my techniques.

Fellow Barbadians, I trust some of what I said today will be remembered and practiced and will bring forth fruit.

"We are not divided, all one body we, one in faith; in hope, in doctrine, one in charity".

My word to you today is, assist in the great work he is doing and help complete this magnificent task.

10. South Africa, Land of Opportunity

2005

Forty two anticipatory souls left for South Africa via London, some as missionaries, some as tourists or some just having a summer break. From the sky, South Africa is a thing of beauty and when one touches the ground, it seems to touch paradise. We spent the first two weeks of July touring the southern-most country on the continent of Africa. We landed first in Cape Town on the south-western coast and were welcomed by the majestic Table Mountain, we all had learned about in secondary school. Table Mountain is so called because it is flat on the top like the top of a mesa (the Spanish for table),

We hired a tour bus and tour guide for our stay. Our guide was a beautiful native of Namibia (formerly South-West Africa). The guide was a linguist and a historian. We were lucky to have two such persons on board. The guide was a person of mixed race and our driver Charles, was of Indian descent. It is important knowing this as under apartheid all the races lived separate. No province more typified apartheid than Cape Town. In Cape Town, the area was divided into districts and the districts were peopled along racial lines. There were districts for Indians, Coloreds, Anglos, Afrikaans, and the Blacks (native Africans) lived in the ghettos, euphemistically called townships.

In 1954 a law was passed mandating the separation of races. In Cape Town, there was an integrated district, called District Six. This district was integrated for years and could have been the world's first model of successful multi-racial living. But the bull dozers moved in and put an end to this experiment. All the buildings were erased except for a Catholic and a Moravian Church. This is one of South Africa's tales of man's inhumanity to man.

During the day we toured and encamped at night, From Cape Town we visited Table Mountain, Boulders (home of the penguins)

and Robben Island where Nelson Mandela was unjustly imprisoned for twenty seven years. Today Robben Island is only a museum and a must for all visitors to South Africa and one must see Cell No. 5, Mandela's home for all those years. From Cape Town, we stopped off in Oudtshoorn, home for many wild animals and wild life reserves. At one reserve, we were even allowed to pat a tame cheetah. Another exciting stop was an ostrich farm where some rode ostriches. There was even an ostrich race. One has to see ostriches to really understand their enormous size.

After a few days in Oudtshoorn, we traveled further eastwards to Knysa, another unbelievably beautiful city. There we visited the world famous Cango caves with their awesome undulating chambers. If that was not enough we had time to visit some of the world's richest wineries. Not known to many, South Africa is the producer of some of the world's best wines. From Knysa, we went further east to George with its beautiful lagoons and vocational islands for the rich. As pre-arranged we flew from George to Johannesburg. Here we were again reminded of the extreme wealth on one hand and the extreme poverty on the other. It is unrealistic to think this can be reversed over-night.

From Johannesburg, we visited Soweto, the biggest and best-known township. Soweto was and continues to be home of both Mandela's and fellow Nobel peace prize winner, his eminence, Arch-Bishop Tutu. From Johannesburg, we resumed our bus tour, first visiting the captivating Soweto and finally Pretoria, the capital of South Africa, the former home of Peter Krueger, founder of the modern South Africa and the early architect of apartheid.

South Africa is a vast country, rich in resources and opportunities. South Africa can become the home of many blacks of the Diaspora and give them the opportunity to become first class citizens in a first-class country. Now I shall like to reflect on what I saw and learned in those two weeks in July.

First, let us look at the downside. Wherever one went one saw the vestiges of apartheid. One saw most blacks doing the hard work, the menial and under-paid jobs. High schools were mostly boarding schools and outside the townships thus holding down the number capable of moving upwards. Rome, it is said, was not built in a day, neither can apartheid be dismantled in a day. Next, and this is the most painful part of our tour, namely child prostitution and the devastating spread of H.I.V./A.I.D.S.; and of these over one million are children who will never see their teens. Our hearts cry out for these young and innocent victims, who will not live to see South Africa become great. We in the Diaspora must do more to help South Africa. They alone cannot whip this problem.

Now for the upside: South Africa is perhaps the most westernized of African countries and has a fairly high percentage of educated blacks, who do not believe in turning their backs on their own, but believe in giving something back. This is a virtue that should be encouraged.

Finally, the greatest lesson, South Africa is teaching the world is called Reconciliation. South Africans have rightly decided there is no time nor room for vengeance, only for Reconciliation, Peace and Love.

11. Black History Lecture

<u>**2000**</u>

A few years ago I had to introduce a beautiful sister and missed and referred to her as a Jamaican. Did she go apoplectic? Did she let me have it? The sister said Professor Gill, "If you want to describe me, won't you first ask me?" I have never made this mistake since. Not only did it teach me a lesson, it got me to do some serious thinking. I have visited over twenty countries, been a legal resident in four and a citizen of two. This has allowed me to see persons of color living in different countries, sometimes as the Majority, as here in the West Indies, and sometimes in the Minority and in each of these the behaviors, histories, cultures and assimilations have been different.

This has led me to ask "Why is this so?" What characteristics seem to be similar and which ones dissimilar? This is my latest field of interest and study. This subject matter is so vast, so challenging and so controversial, that it may take up all my remaining time; but I am determined to begin and if I cannot complete it, I pray to God to let me motivate some young person to get interested, to get involved, to lend me a hand, especially with typing and research. If there are any members of this audience interested in this, please see me at the end and get my particulars.

We first have to define the subject matter of interest, establish parameters, linguistics, methodologies and so on. We must rise above narrow and petty semantics and allow the need for and the importance of the study and only that dictate the course and rate of our progress. Members of the African Diaspora need to know this and for authenticity only members of the Diaspora to work on the study. Not only will it involve much study and research, it will also involve much travelling. Not only travel to different countries but also much travelling within each specific country.

Many members of the Diaspora may physically look alike but their histories and experiences vastly differ. When I visited South Africa, this observation hit me forcefully. How could people who racially look alike, think and act so dissimilarly and in some instances contradictorily? So fellow Africans, there you have it; you can see the enormity and complexity of the task. It is daunting, herculean but very important. Why are Africans from the West coast so different from those on the East coast? Within one country, e.g. South Africa, why would people in one region be so different from those in another? Why are the descendants of African slaves be so different from Africans not sold into slavery? Why would the descendants of African slaves, say in Brazil, be different to those in Haiti or say Jamaica? Why do Barbadians think and act different from Afro-Americans born in Mississippi and so on? It is these dissimilarities and disparities that prevent us from being seen as a monolithic group on the world stage. Friends it will take more than the commonality of skin color to bring people of color together.

For people to be regarded as a major player, they must not only look alike, but start to think, behave, act and react alike. To accelerate this unity will call for a major language or languages learned and spoken, a new religion, still believing in a Supreme Hunan Being but endowing Africans in history with the attributes of the God Head which Caucasians have captured and have the prophets, religious scholars and even Jesus. When young Africans in Africa and the Diaspora see Adam and Eve, Moses, David, Solomon, Joseph, Mary and Jesus as persons of color that would revolutionize our behaviors and self-worth.

To be taken seriously and to regain positions of greatness, which people of color once enjoyed, we must act like a great people, like a serious people like our ancestors who were the first people God created. That means stop copying and imitating a sub-species that split off from the major species, the Negroid race, the only race that God created. You can run home to your P.C.s and Google and confirm this assertion. The other two major groups of mankind are not races, they are called Sub-Species, because they came out of the major group, the Negroid race. These sup-species are the Caucasoids (referring to the people of Caucasian expression that look white, but are not really white.) The second sub-species are called the Mongoloid sub-species and as their name suggests these are mixed and are mainly the yellow or Asiatic peoples: Chinese, Japanese, Koreans, Thai etc.

So fellow Africans, we are a special people; we are the only people that can be called a race. To use the words of the late Great Hon. Marcus Mosiah Garvey "Rise you mighty people, Great you are and Great you will be again". Wherever we are remember (repeat) Remember that we are Africans, not Afro-anything. We are Africans either living in Africa or in the Diaspora. It is only when this happens, will we cease being disparate, fragmented groups and emerge once again as a race; the race created by God and described in Genesis Ch. 1 and 2. The Holy Bible is the only authoritative source for the validity of what I just said. Remember that there is but one race and two sub-groupings called Sub-species.

The only other thing I shall like to add is the word "Africa", should be spelled with a K not a C so it would read "Afrika". Do not perpetuate the incorrect spelling of Caucasians. Brothers we have a great work cut out to do. Cut out the jitterbugging, the copying, the imitating of less great people. Young people here is a project in which you can be involved – an after school activity, namely researching what we were, the fall from greatness and come up with a proposal to make us a Great Race as intoned by Hon. Marcus Mosiah Garvey and always remember these two things: (1) We are the only race and were created by God and (2) just as important, We were made in the image of God (Again see Genesis Ch. 1 & 2).

I shall like to leave these few words of Tennyson with you.

"The old order changeth to new

And God reveals himself in many ways

Lest the old corrupt the new."

Ladies and gentlemen, fellow Africans, thank you. We have great work to do Please let us begin. GOD BLESS YOU.

SECTION III
Religious

1. To Be a Christian Is to Be Color-Blind

1966

I recently recalled a poem I learned as a boy. It was called "The Blind Boy" by Henry Longfellow. In it, the poet wrote, "My day or night myself I make whene'er I sleep or play."

I sometimes wish we could all be like that when it comes to the question of skin color, then we could judge our fellow beings without any reference to the irrelevant consideration of skin color.

I recommend that we all reread the excerpt from Bishop Oliver Maynard's (EWI) speech to the Missionary Conference, in Winston Salem last November (May Pine and Palm issue on page 10). In it the Bishop says "To accept one another as Christ has accepted us, is a very different matter. It is through Jesus Christ that we receive new direction for our lives…and are enabled to break through our self-centered limitations and prejudices…" In other words he is telling us that to be a Christian is to be color-blind.

We should explore the myth that one skin color is superior to another. The reasons that racists usually give for their belief in this myth are: (1) genetic, (2) economic superiority. Both of these are without merit.

(1) Genetic superiority – Whenever two parents of the same skin color perform the procreative act, it follows as night the day that their offspring will be of the same skin color. This is what biologists call truism.

(2) Economic superiority – The countries of Western Europe and here in North America were the first to be industrialized because they acquired a leap start in the acquisition of material goods. Today we are seeing this gap becoming smaller as the poorer nations also become industrialized.

We can therefore see how faulty are the foundations of the myth of racial superiority. On the other hand, Christians as truly color-blind persons can confidently say "On Christ the solid rock I stand, all other ground is sinking sand."

As Moravians and the world's first missionaries, we do not have too bad a record in the area of race relations, but in the opinion of this writer we need to improve in the following areas: (1) the way in which the present call system is exercised, (2) the reticence of our congregations to accept pastors of another skin color or culture; (3) the reticence of similar congregations in accepting members whose color or culture may be different from their own.

Having stated my observations, here are some recommendations to help overcome the above shortcomings: (1) revise the call system to make it truly color-blind; (2) develop a system of exchanging pastors for short stays with different color congregations; (3) each congregation to adopt a different color congregation and by means of exchange visits help to develop a greater closeness in Christ; (4) establish a provincial commission on equal justice and human rights for equal justice at home and full human rights abroad.

In 1954, the U.S. Supreme Court, in its Brown vs Topeka (Brown vs Board of Education) decision, rejected the Plessey Doctrine of separate but equal and our church could be the first major denomination to go on record as also rejecting the separate but equal doctrine. This should be easy to do if we but remember "to be a Christian is to be color-blind."

As Moravians we have a great history and could have an even greater future, if we could become a truly color-blind Unity.

In Christ there is no East or West, in him no South or North.

P. 15 of "The Moravian Monthly Magazine of The Moravian Church, U.S.A.

November 1986.

2. No Room in the Inn

'Twas a cold December night in 1987, when a young unemployed man called Jose and his teenage wife Maria rode up and down in the 'F' train in New York City, because they had nowhere to stay, not even in the crumbling, vermin-infested, welfare hotels.

In New York City alone there are some fifty thousand homeless people and nation-wide about two million, in our nation of plenty. The problem perhaps would be greater, were it not for the actions of the churches in helping to alleviate the plight of the needy and homeless.

We cannot rely on government alone to solve the problems of hunger and homelessness. Here are things we can consider as Christian congregations:

- As a long term solution, follow the exemplary lead of First Moravian of New York City and try to provide permanent housing by either erecting or renovating existing housing stock.
- Establish a nightly shelter, staffed by volunteers and a lot of good will.
- Help to alleviate the hunger by establishing facilities such as a soup kitchen or a food pantry, either alone or in cooperation with other congregations.

As individual Christians, these are some of the things we can do:

*Be a volunteer in our own church or some neighboring church with its own sheltering program.

*Donate money and/or clothing for the poor, in particular for the children.

*Donate some time as well as gifts of food and/or money for a soup kitchen or food pantry at either your own church or a sister church.

One of the greatest ways in which we can celebrate this coming of our Lord in this new year is to do something positive about the poverty in our midst, so that there will be fewer Joses and Marias riding the subways all night in our inner cities.

The Moravian December 1987

3. Dr. King's Dream

This quotation was taken not from a political platform but from "The Moravian Covenant for Christian Living", formerly known as "The Brotherly Agreement". This document, like the Sermon on the Mount and the Martin Luther King, Jr's teachings (especially his "I Have A Dream", delivered in Washington in 1963) should be made compulsory reading. As we honor the memory of this saint on his birthday, January 15, - belatedly made U.S.A. holiday – may we celebrate by resolving to make his dream come true.

Fellow Moravians, let us take an honest look at the state of race relations, first in the United States and then in our church.

The world including the United States, is a better place than in 1963. The Civil Right Acts are part of the law of the land. *Brown vs Board of Education* is still unscathed despite many assaults upon it. Martin Luther King Jr would have included in his dream the desegregation of churches and an end to apartheid in South Africa.

However, in spite of improved race relations, racism is still alive and rearing its ugly head. One only has to read the letters to the editor in the daily papers and our Moravian to know this is so.

Only an acceptance of our Lord Jesus and an unconditional acceptance of our common humanity will bring about the death knoll of racism. As Christians we must steadfastly believe that "as in Adam all die, so also in Christ shall all be made alive". (I Corinthians 15:22). The Anglican Archbishop of South Africa said, "We are all made in the image of God." And he added that this included both him and Prime Minister Botha.

Moravian Bishop Oliver Maynard has aptly put it: "We belong to each other because of Jesus Christ: so let us accept one another unconditionally in Jesus Christ." Only when we do this will we cease to have race-related incidents such as those that occurred in Forsyth County, G.A. and Robeson County, N.C.; Howard Beach and Staten Island, N.Y.

This brings us to the state of race relations in the Unitas Fratrum here in North America. Sad to say, we still have segregated congregations and not one Caucasian church has ever accepted a pastor of a different color. The U.S. Supreme court in *Brown* vs. Board of Education said that "separate is inherently unequal." This writer hastens to add, "It is also inherently un-Christian." We show that we do not sincerely believe that we are one as God's children when we discriminate on the grounds of race, color and national origin.

What can we as Moravians do? We can make sure that the leaders we elect are persons of vision who will not pay lip service to equality but instead will lead and inspire us to practice it.

Our Moravian forebears were not afraid to believe in and practice equality. Dober and Nitschmann were not afraid to practice it. We must recapture the zeal and conviction of those early missionaries if we want to be known as a Christian denomination and not as a white one.

The picture is not entirely a bleak one. We still have some silver linings, such as a number of integrated churches and a great number of Moravians who are willing to worship and pray with all persons. The more we become a color-blind church, the stronger will our witness be. Jesus said, "I come that they might have life and have it more abundantly" (John10:10 KJV) Fellow Moravians, the practice of racism only thwarts our Christian growth and prevents us from enjoying that more abundant life which Jesus promised.

4. Sermon

The First Word

By Brother C. Alfie Gill (Elder)
Good Friday April 18, 2003

Have you forgiven anyone today? Well I have. First the Long Island Railroad was late, (as usual). Secondly City Buses.

There are two sides to this word – First, Jesus is asking his father to forgive his enemies. (2) He makes excuses for them. "For they know not what they do." Yes, if they did, they would not be crucifying him. They thought they were crucifying a mere man, the son of Joseph the Carpenter and Mary, but I have different news, they were crucifying the son of God. For that heresy, they need God's forgiveness, just like you and I today. What do we ask God to do, every time we say the Lord's prayer?

We say "forgive us etc…" Divine forgiveness demands complete satisfaction to meet the demands of God's outraged holiness, See Romans Ch. 3-v24 and Acts Ch. 17- v30. In the Old Testament, a lamb was slaughtered as the covering for sin and guess what? Lambs had to be constantly slaughtered, By the way, they always gave one a chance to escape and what was that one called? A 'scape goat.' That is the origin of that expression. But, when Jesus came, this slaughter of the innocents stopped and Jesus became the propitiation for our sins. (Deut. 21)

Brothers and Sisters, "Forgiveness" is something to practice not merely talk about. One of the disciples (?) once asked Jesus "How often must I forgive a transgressor?" Shall it be seven times seven? Jesus answered "not seven times seven, but seventy times seven." In other words, as much as it takes. (John Ch. 3-v14-21). To forgive means to wipe the slate clean. If the slate is wiped clean, then there is nothing to remember. You know some people say, "I forgive you, but I can't forget." What that person is really saying is…. "I haven't forgiven you."

This Moravian Church started because a Catholic priest in Prague stood up to the Pope and let the Catholic authorities know that only God can forgive sins. No Pope, no priest can forgive sins. (Amen)

I want to do this exercise. Close your eyes if you want. Now imagine Jesus on the cross. "See from His head, His hands, His feet - etc…" Yes Brothers and Sisters, that's what this Good Friday is about. I Want you to say with me this quotation: "To err is human, to forgive is divine." Isn't that good news, Amen. Now in closing, boys and girls and adults as well…..

"There is s Green hill far away/Without a city wall/Where our dear Lord was crucified/Who died to save us all."

"He died that we might be forgiven./ He died to make us good./ That we might go at last to heaven/ Saved by his precious blood."

Closing Prayer

5. The Second Word

Brother C. Alfie Gill

April 9, 2004

I do not know if any of you came from any country with a town, a village or even a beach called Paradise, Well in Barbados we have some and believe me, they are like Paradise, areas of unbelievable beauty and heavenly rest.

On the south-eastern coast of Barbados, we have such an area, it is called Paradise Heights and the neighboring beach is called Paradise Beach. The houses are dream houses, of magnificent beauty and well-manicured lawns. Believe me Brothers and Sisters, if you visit Barbados you will want to see Paradise Heights. But today I am going to refer you to even a superior, more beautiful, more tranquil Paradise that is the one Jesus is offering us, that is the one Jesus offered the thief on the cross. To receive Jesus' invitation like the thief, you must turn away from your evil ways. You must say "Lord have mercy on me a miserable sinner". One thief reviled and scoffed at Jesus, the other asserted Jesus' innocence and his own guilt; for this he earned Jesus' forgiveness and an invitation "Today you will be with me in Paradise". Brothers and Sisters that most desired, long-for invitation (I don't know about you) but I would like to receive such an invitation.

For a few brief moments, we shall like to analyze this passage of scripture. There are three aspects to look at. (1) One is his emphasis on today. (today, not tomorrow) The other two are (2) What is Paradise? And (3) Where is it?

Why today? Now is the accepted time, today is the day of salvation. (Amen Somebody). You know the old saying "Don't put off for tomorrow, that which can be done today", here is one thing all of us can do today. Today, (before this day is over), and that is accept

75

Jesus as our personal savior, confess our sins and in return believe in (1) His forgiveness and (2) receive a bonus, namely to meet with him in Paradise. (Amen)

What is Paradise? Paradise is a rest stop on your way to heaven. Heaven is our goal, our final destination. There in Paradise you shed your worldly clothes, earthly habits and you get ready to enter Heaven. Where is Paradise? It certainly is not in Barbados or any earthly place. Paradise, dear friends, is wherever Jesus is. On the Great Saturday his body lay in the tomb and his spirit lay in Paradise. Remember Jesus did not enter Heaven until forty days later, on the day of Ascension. (see Acts Ch. 1 v9-11)

"He died that we might be forgiven. He died to make us good, that we might go at last to Heaven, saved by his precious blood".

Jesus is calling on us today "Repent and be baptized". He assures us "in my father's house there are many mansions, if it were not so I would have told you" (John14 v1-3). One sign you will never see on Heaven's gate is "NO ROOM". Dear friends let's use these Good Fridays to get closer to Jesus, closer to Heaven. Say with me "Jesus keep me near the cross, there is a precious fountain, till my ruptured soul shall find, rest beyond the river".

Let us find solace in John 3 v16. Do not let Jesus die in vain, Accept him today, promise to give up the things not pleasing in his sight, let us love one another until we make Heaven our home. As John Milton wrote many years ago, "We may lose Paradise, but it can be regained". What a precious thought? Are you listening? Will you take the first step? Jesus is calling. Will you answer?

(Prayer)

6. The Third Word – "Woman Behold Thy Son"

Good Friday. March 29, 2002

In 1989 a mother became very ill. Her son, who was overseas, rushed home to be with her. The time came when he had to return overseas. He could not bear to see her alone; hence he hired a private nurse to be with her five days per week and for close relatives to fill in on the weekends. That was that son's way of following Jesus' command "Son behold thy mother".

Our message therefore has a two-fold aspect:

(1) a mother's love for her child and

(2) children's love for mother.

For mother's love, we shall rely heavily on the New Testament and for a child's reciprocal love for mother we shall go to no better authority than the Old Testament.

What does the 5th commandment command us? (*pause*) Why? (*pause*)

There you have it boys and girls, brothers and sisters. The Bible commands us to love our parents. If you ask brother Roberts or any of our seniors the secret for their longevity, they will tell you – (a) Love of God and the love of mother, when they were young and if you ask mother, her greatest satisfaction, she would tell you unashamedly "Loving those children of mine". There is no love Brothers and Sisters you know, to equal that of a mother's. Yes love for a spouse comes close, but never equals. You can divorce your spouse, can't you? But whoever heard of divorcing his or her mother?

One of my late mother's favorite hymns was an Anglican one which started as follows: "Can a mother's tender care cease toward the one she bear?" Yes boys and girls, in life you will meet many people, but none equal to mother.

My late mother was an amazing person. Not only did she write her own funeral program (hymns etc. and Psalms 46). She also wrote her own eulogy, leaving me the easy task of reading it. The only thing I added was a poem I composed called "The Best Mother". The last two lines read like this: "In heaven a noble work was done, when God gave me my mother."

Yes dear friends, this is what this third word is all about - a mother's unbounding love for her children and their reciprocal love for mother. In the West Indies we have a saying: "A child may not know who his/her father is but every child knows who his/her mother is."

Can a mother's tender care cease? No Brothers and Sisters, not even by those who drown their kids in the bath, for they protest their innocence by saying the devil made me do it.

Could Jesus' love ever cease for Mary his mother? Never, because it was to her the angel said "Blessed art thou amongst women, and blessed is the fruit of thy womb, Jesus." (Alleluia)

Jesus is our perfect role model. There he is on Calvary's cross just moments away from death and what is he doing? Making a living will, providing for mother.

1) To John. "Behold thy mother"
    He is also providing for John.
2) "Woman behold thy son."

Even the thief on the cross he makes provision for, "today thou shalt be with me in Paradise."

That is not all Brothers and Sisters. He also made provision for you and me. Jesus says "I go to prepare a place for you, that where I am, you may be also.

Jesus says "in my father's house are many mansions. If it were not so, I would have told you." Yes Brothers and Sisters, our Jesus does not lie; he is building mansions. That is what this Good Friday is all about. God's unilateral, often unrequited love for us.

John 3:16 put it correctly. Amen.

In the Barbershop I go to get my hair cut, recently someone asked if Mary was the Mother of God. The argument was "If Mary was the mother of Jesus and Jesus was God, as they say in Geometry, therefore Mary was also the Mother of God."

But I have news for you. God is a spirit and a spirit does not need a father or a mother. Let us turn to John Chapter 1:1-14.

So there you have it, Mary was the mother of Jesus in human flesh, but was never and could never be the mother of God. God is a spirit and they that worship him must do so in spirit and in truth.

The message therefore this afternoon is that Christ died for Mary. He also died for you and me.

"There was no other good enough to pay the price of sin. Only Jesus could unlock the gate of heaven and let us in."

(Prayer)

7. The Sixth Word – "It is Finished"

Good Friday - April 2, 1999

Brothers and sisters in about ten minutes our pastor our pastor is going to look at me and then at his watch and I shall interpret his body language to mean "your time is up, kindly wrap up".

My late mother used to manage a bakery and Mother baked the best rum cake in the world. I remember her taking it out, inhaling the fumes, testing it and announcing proudly, **"It is finished"**. You sisters in particular, at Thanksgiving, you take that turkey from the oven, you test it and announce, **"It is finished"**.

Michelangelo, on completion of his great painting of the ceiling in the Sistine Chapel, sighed and announced, **"It is finished"**. Those three words usually announce the completion of a task, sometimes well done, or sometimes not so well done, but always in a note of finality; or as the French would say, it is a "fait accompli".

At a recent funeral here, our closing hymn was **"Servant of God, well done"**. Likewise on that Good Friday more than two thousand years ago, Jesus is approaching the end of his ministry and his earthly struggle. St. Luke captures those moments as Jesus contemplates the approaching end. Luke tells us in Luke 22:44, that he perspired so heavily as if drops of blood. He asks his heavenly Father to take the cup from him, he tells his Father "it is not my will Lord, but let your will be done". Jesus Christ had completed his earthly mission. He had lived 33 years without sin, showing that it was possible. He yielded not into temptation because yielding would have been a sin. Why linger when his task is over? Jesus needed to cast off his mortal flesh because it is written, **"flesh and blood cannot enter into eternal life"**. Yes, that first Good Friday, Jesus did two things at the same time. (1) Gave up the earthly body and (2) died that we might be forgiven. He died to make us good, yes it was finished. He had fought the good fight. Jesus had kept the faith. For him there was no shortcut, no cheating.

In one marathon a few years ago, one female runner was declared the winner only to have the title taken away the next day. Apparently someone saw her leave the course, take the subway and near the finish line re-enter the race fresh and declared the winner. Friends there are no shortcuts. Jesus said, "I am the way the truth and the life. If any man comes to the father he must come through me". We are exhorted to fight the good fight with all our might and also run the straight race through God's good grace. Our fight must be clean, not as in one fight a few years ago when one fighter tried to bite off the ear of another. Dear friends this race is about endurance. The race is not for the swift but for those who endure to the end. Just as Jesus did in the Garden of Gethsemane. Luke 22:44, He put his whole faith into God's hands with the words, "**Father into your hands I commend my spirit**". Jesus was going to let God become the pilot and lead him successfully past death and into eternal life. We too must leave it to Jesus, for there was no other good enough to pay the price of sin. Only Jesus can unlock the gate of heaven and let us in.

St. Paul too entered the race. First he was headed in the wrong direction, then God turned him around so much so that in Paul's "garden of agony", when approaching the end, he proudly announced, "**I have fought a good fight, I have finished my course, I have kept the faith**". Paul wrote in his letter to Timothy, Chapter 4:7. Dear Friend this race needs not be in vain, because Jesus has assured us in John 14:2. "In my father's house there are many mansions. If it were not so I would have told you. Behold I go to prepare a place for you". Isn't that a pleasant thought that death and eternal separation from God need not be the end? A real possibility of occupying one of these mansions in the hereafter exists.

Dear friend can you endure to the end? Are you willing to finish the race and keep the faith? If you do, you too could be greeted hereafter with the words, "**Servant of God, well done. Enter into the joy of love**". **Will you be ready?**

Think on these things.

Shall we bow our heads in prayer?

Heavenly Father, this Good Friday we pray for a world not at peace. Where there is war, make peace. Where there is disunity, sow unity. Heal churches that are divided and families that are broken.

> "Lord, teach me to be generous,
> to serve you as you deserve,
> to give and not to count the cost,
> to fight and not to heed the wounds,
> to toil and not to seek for rest,
> to labor and not to look for any reward,
> save that of knowing that I do your holy will".

Finally, let us show forth thy praise not only with our lips, but in our lives, by giving up ourselves to thy service and by walking before thee in righteousness all our days. This we ask in the name of Jesus Christ our crucified and resurrected savior. Amen.

8. Sermon

August 22, 1998

Greetings. Welcome. It is nine days since Moravians celebrated the August 13th experience of 1727 and today is also the 12th Sunday after Pentecost. Our text for today will spawn both of these events as they have so much in common. Let us read together from John 14:12-18 and Acts 1:4; 16-18.

First we have an example of an all-wise God who knows our needs before we ask and our ignorance in asking. Many of you are parents and if you had to leave home for some time, you would tell your young ones, "I shall not leave you comfortless. I have asked Aunt Kath to take care of you when I am gone".

Likewise, God always keeps his promises, even when we don't see them. So on the first Pentecost, two thousand years ago, the promise that God will not leave us comfortless became true. (Acts 1:16-18) Yes friends, when one is full of the Holy Spirit, one can prophesy. Yes, one can see visions and one can even speak in tongues. Maybe we haven't seen much of this lately since so few can be said to be filled with the Holy Spirit.

Now let us jump 1700 years in history. The Hussites, or the followers of John Hus were decimated by wars, disease and other attrition. Let me read you the footnote of the daily text for August 13. (Quote)

Yes, this outpouring of the Holy Spirit saved those worshipers at Berthelsforf, Germany and thus marks the renewal of the Unitas Fratrum or modern Moravian Church.

Before we go on, why this Holy Spirit? The Holy Spirit is the Third person of the Blessed trinity; first there is God the creator, next Jesus, the Redeemer and thirdly the Holy Spirit who is called the Comforter by Jesus in our text.

In Acts Chapter 4:31 "And when they (Peter and the imprisoned apostles) had prayed the place was shaken…and they were filled with the Holy Spirit and they spoke the word of God with boldness".

Yes my friends, speaking the word of God with boldness is the hallmark of one that is filled with the Holy Spirit. When the Holy Spirit fills you, you cannot stay quiet. You want to proclaim the word of God and above all you want to live a spirit-filled life "so that in you, people may see the good works of God and they too would want to glorify our father who is in heaven". A Christian is without doubt a spirit-filled person. We Moravians do not practice adult baptism but the churches that do, say that when one is submerged and when one gets up, that person has the Holy Spirit. Whether we practice adult baptism or not, the question as Moravians would say – "This is a non-essential". What is more important, is that the person undergoes an inward change which is then exemplified by the way that he or she lives? Yes, the Bible says, "by their fruits, you shall know them".

Next, how can we today receive the Holy Spirit? My answer is this: Get down on your knees (and I mean knees) and pray with your heart and soul, cry out to God, "Lord have mercy upon me, a sinner" and as you are down there on your knees surrender your heart to God. Cry "All to Jesus I surrender" and believe me friends that is the equivalent of any adult Baptism, when you get up off your knees and as you go about your daily living, people will observe the Holy Spirit working in you. To young ones, here is a prayer you can add to your other prayers. Say after me "do no sinful action, speak no angry word, we belong to Jesus, Children of the Lord".

Dear friends, within the last month I attended three funerals. All three were suddenly called home like young john F. Kennedy, his wife and sister-in-law and I could not but hope that they were ready. Dear friend, suppose you were suddenly called home today, would you be ready? I ask this question in all seriousness. To be ready we must accept Jesus as our personal Saviour. We must invite the Holy Spirit to enter into our lives and let our light shine before others. If we haven't done this, I mean in all seriousness, we should consider doing so, not tomorrow but today. Let today be your day of Pentecost.

Let the Holy Spirit fill you as it did those early Moravians. Yes dear friends, do not put this off for one day. Sister Tulip Greenidge in going to her car was cut down; young Kennedy, on July 16, was plucked from the sky. This is a decision, dear friend, that should be made today, for now is the accepted time, today is the day of salvation. As the poet Longfellow put it, "Not enjoyment and not sorrow is our destined end or way, but to live that each tomorrow finds us far better than today".

I do not intend to scare anyone, but I would like us to reflect on how suddenly it could be all over, as it was for Sister Lesanne, Sister Francis and Sister Greenidge. I do not know about you, but every time I go to a funeral, I say the following prayer: "Thank you dear Lord that this funeral is not mine, but let thy Holy Spirit lead me to a better life, so that I will be ready when you do call me". In my family too, I have experienced sudden loss and believe me it is not easy. On Friday, November 22, 1968, I called Barbados to wish my only nephew a happy 16th birthday, only to be told that they had just returned from his funeral, caused by his drowning two days earlier. For years I reflected on Tony's death and came to the conclusion, that God needs angels of all ages, shapes and sizes, and that God needed my nephew to be an angel to help welcome other young people, He may call 'home'. Yes dear friend, we can be here today and gone tomorrow. If we are going to invite the Holy Spirit, let it be today, for tomorrow may be too late. Now I invite all of you to recite with me the first and second verses of the hymn "Come Holy Ghost, our soul inspire".

Shall we bow our heads in prayer?

PRAYER

9. Sermon At United Moravian Church, NY On Sunday, April 21, 2002.

Let us read together from St. John Chapter 3:13-17. I am sorry to disappoint anyone who was looking forward to some highfaluting, highbrow sermon. This is going to be a very explicit sermon on one of the greatest, most basic needs of our time – LOVE. (L.O.V.E.) Short, simple but importantly most lacking. I would say most confidently that with love we could solve nearly all the world's problems. The lion and the lamb could lie down together; Jews and Arabs could stop killing each other and the various races would stop hating and discriminating against each other. The prophet Isaiah said "they could beat their swords into plough-shares and their spears into pruning hooks and there should be war no more". (Isaiah Ch. 24:44) Wouldn't that be a blessed day when we could truly sing "down by the riverside and study war no more"?

It was thought that after the fall of communism, peace would be ushered in and we would have what was known as the peace dividend. That is, all the money saved from making bombs, would be used for schools, health care etc., but that just did not happen. Brothers and Sisters, another word for peace is love. Next time we pass the peace, think of what you are really saying, "My love to you". I think love has a more personal ring to it than the word 'peace'.

I don't know how many of you ever read the novel "Love Story" by Eric Seigel or have seen the movie. However that movie gave my favorite definition for love; namely, "Love is never having to say you are sorry". Isn't that true Brothers and Sisters? God never has to say He is sorry. (John 3:16)

My second favorite definition for love is found in Corinthians. Let us read together I Corinthians Ch. 13:1-13.

So you see why I chose "Love" as my theme this morning. There is a song with beautiful words called: "What the world needs now

86

is love, sweet love" or what about this one from Jamaica sung by Bob Marley "One love, one heart, etc". I am going to give you some homework to do. Ready?

1. See how many songs or Hymns you know with 'love' in them.
2. How many verses in the New Testament have the word 'love'?

Love has a three-fold aspect.
1] Love for God. 2] Self. 3] Neighbor

Love for God (see Luke 10:27) "Love God with all your heart etc." Here what the Good Book says, "If you say you love God, but don't love your neighbor, etc" Strong words, but true.

Peace: <u>Hymn</u>

"Let there be peace on earth
And let it begin with me.
Let there be peace on earth
The peace that was meant to be".

Secondly: A lot of the world's problems come from self-hate. If someone doesn't love himself or herself, how can he or she love you? Low self-esteem is a sign of self-hate. With high self-esteem, namely love for oneself, we can create a new person.

Thirdly: Love for someone else (your neighbor). Who is your neighbor? The parable of the Good Samaritan gave the answer and what was it Brothers and Sisters?

The answer, is 'one who shows compassion'. Let that be your creed. (Luke Ch 10:25-37).

Yes, for God so loved the world etc. (John 3:16). Jesus loves us Brothers and Sisters and did this much for us. What shall we do for him? Silver and gold have I none but such as I have, give I thee:" Acts Ch 3:6.

So to sum up this message, we go back to I Corinthians Ch. 13:13. Remember Jesus loved us and died for us. What shall we do for him? Remember for peace on earth "let it begin with me".

PRAYER

10. Letter to The Editor

Prof. C. Alfie Gill, N.P, LL.B., MB.A.
PO Box 4085
Hempstead, NY 11551

July 31, 2000
The Moravian
Att. Ms. Miller (Editor)
PO Box 1245
Bethlehem, PA 18016-1245

Dear Ms. Miller,

The July edition of "The Moravian left me astounded, on page 29. First you printed the letter of a reader who has become an ex-reader" because of an intolerant article on Buddhism in a former issue.

Then to show you did not get the message, you proceeded to print (also on the same page) the meanest most bigoted article that ever appeared in your pages. I call the letter of your reader (L. James Harvey, PhD.) bigoted, because he berated (if not slandered) a lady of color who is doing the same thing as thousands of Caucasian celebrities, without bringing down your reader's wrath.

Has he ever read the story in the Bible (John 8:7) of Jesus' encounter with the woman caught in adultery? I offer your letter-writer the same advice Jesus offered, namely, "let him that is without sin cast the first stone".

How would your (Holier Than Thou) letter-writer have characterized the relationship between Mary and Joseph before the birth of Jesus?

For the information of your letter-writer, this unjustly criticized lady has given more than ten million dollars to Better Chance and other organizations to help gifted but impoverished students. Actions speak louder than words.

Our denomination though small, has a sizable number of minorities and these find the letter of your correspondent quite offensive, (and maybe an encouragement to also become ex-readers (?) of your Magazine.)

Sincerely,
Prof. C. Alfie Gill (C.U.N.Y.)
United Moravian Church of New York

11. Letter to The Editor

Moravian Magazine April 1992

I urge you to correct the false impression in the letter [by Dr. Jud in April1992] that all Moravians are over-enamored with Capitalism. All Moravians and all Americans are not. Your correspondent was speaking merely for himself.

Communism was an evil and rightly deserved to fall but that does not make capitalism a better system.

What is so great about a system that has produced two world wars in our time, countless mini-wars, the loss of millions of lives and countless billions in property damage? What is so great about a system, that every few years gives us recessions and yes, the 'Great Depression', not to speak of the homeless, hungry and unemployed that exist in the U.S.A. right now?

Let Dr. Lewis [writer of the article to which Dr. Jud's letter was a response] be assured that many Moravians and Americans are hoping for and striving for a more Christian, fairer and more humane system.

12. Letter to The Editor

Prof. C. Alfie Gill, N.P, LL.B., MB.A.
PO Box 4085
Hempstead, NY 11551

July 31, 2000

The Moravian
Att. Ms. Miller
PO Box 1245
Bethlehem, PA 18016-1245

Dear Ms. Miller,

I trust you can publish in a future issue my reflection on the recently held synod of the Eastern District.

I was a Delegate from New York, who arrived on Wednesday night, June 14th about 8p.m., only to find that the most important offices had already been voted upon.

That was only to be my first disappointment. Over three days, the only two issues to generate any heat were: 1) Compassion for homosexuals 2) a defeated resolution calling for criminal background checks for Sunday schools teachers and other youth workers.

Where was the compassion at Synod for the victims of: poverty, injustice, homelessness, exploitation, racism, police-profiling of minorities and difficulty experienced by Moravian minority pastors in getting calls other than to minority churches?

At the beginning of the twenty first century, one would have thought that the Delegates to the Eastern District Synod would have grappled with some of the real problems of the real world. With this benign neglect of the real societal problems, it is no surprise that our denomination continues to be small in size.

I could not help but recall what a former official of the Eastern District once told me. That former official told me that "An Eastern District Synod was more like the Republican Party at prayer" I strongly urge the calling of an interim Eastern District Synod to deal with some or all of the abovementioned and neglected issues. The Parishioners of the Eastern District deserve no less.

Yours in Christ
Prof. C. Alfie Gill – C.U.N.Y
United Moravian Church of New York

13. Eulogy

By Professor Gill

Given in honor of the late JUDGE ERMYN ORVELLA CARRINGTON STROUD on October 30, 2009, the first Afro-American New York City Assistant District Attorney.

Friends, Fellow Africans, Relatives, we come not only to bury Sister Ermyn Orvella, we come also to praise her and if there was ever a mortal worthy of praise, then that person is Ermyn Orvella Stroud. In her 87 years, she achieved more than millions did In one lifetime. She was a loving daughter, then a dutiful wife, loving mother and the most loyal of friends. In everything that Ermyn Orvella did, hers was a first. Among the first mature adults to start a late college and professional career, and wasn't that some career. One of the first Assistant District Attorneys and for fourteen years (1964-1978), she was a fair, able, articulate and strictly professional Assistant District Attorney. She blazed a trail for other Minorities to follow. Be there, females or Africans (her term and mine) for all descendants of those whose fore parents came from the Continent of Africa. She reasoned and so do I that if people from Trinidad, Guyana and other places, whose fore parents came from India or China are called Indians or Chinese why shouldn't those whose fore parents came from Africa, why shouldn't they be called Africans. The word Africans is more correct and uplifting than the word Black and the other words used to degrade and put down persons of color and members of the African Diaspora. The Obituary you are reading describes most beautifully Ermyn the consummate Feminist, Professional and Community Activist, but it does not touch the part of Ermyn's life and which to me, is her real and greatest legacy, namely having all members of the African Diaspora to be called Africans, regardless of the continent, country or island in which they live. Be it on Brazil, with its forty percent African population, be it Jamaica, Barbados or the United

94

States with its sixteen percent African population. Ermyn Orvella, this is a great legacy, a great inestimable contribution to history, one for which we cannot thank you enough.

One of my careers was as a Tax Consultant and one of my first clients was Melody. Like all satisfied clients, she returned the following year and brought some new clients, including her beloved mother. Ermyn and I became friends there and then. Sometimes we lost touch with each other, but never for long and thank the Almighty, never permanently. A few years ago, we reconnected researching the idea that people of color be called Africans regardless of where they live. We found that we were soul-mates and shared passionately some of the same dreams and aspirations, especially that of having us all be called Africans. By extension, those whose forebears came from Europe should be called Europeans or Caucasians, but never by their skin color. I became a friend and consultant to the Ermyn Carrington Stroud Corporation (a Not-For-Profit Corporation) and was busy trying to change the Not-For-Profit to the Ermyn Carrington Stroud Giving Life Foundation. I am therefore throwing this out to the Young Ones present and to the Not-So-Young Ones to help carry on these two dreams of Ermyn Orvella. (1) To bring into being the Foundation and to put into practice, its principles and (2) to enlarge and expand the term "AFRICANS" to mean not only the persons living on the Continent of Africa, but also to all members of the African Diaspora. WHAT A LEGACY? MELODY, you can be truly proud of the achievements of Mom and the expressions of applause shown here this today and forever cherish them.

The English poet, Longfellow, long ago wrote some words which I think are very appropriate to describe Ermyn's life.....

"Lives of great men (and Women) ALL remind us

We can make our lives sublime

And departing, leave behind us.

Footprints on the sands of time"

Sleep on dear Ermyn Orvella. Congrats on your earthly achievements. I am positive that on the Other Side, you will be

greeted with these words, "Well done thou good and faithful servant."
Family, Friends, Fellow Africans, I shall like to leave the words of
a short poem Abou Ben Adhem which I learned in High School, in
Barbados many moons ago. With apologies to the Author I shall like
to re-title it "ERMYN ORVELLA"...

ERMYN ORVELLA

ERMYN ORVELLA, (may her tribe increase!)
Awoke one night from a deep dream of peace,
And saw, within the moonlight in her room,
Making it rich, and like a lily in bloom,
An angel writing in a book of gold:
Exceeding peace had made Ermyn Orvella bold,
And to the Presence in the room she said,
"What writest thou?" The Visitor raised its head,
And with a look made of all sweet accord
Answered, "The names of all those who love the Lord."
"And is mine one?" said Ermyn. "Nay not so,"
Replied the Angel. Ermyn spoke more low,
But cheerily still, and said, "I pray thee then,
Write me as one who loves her fellow men."

The Angel wrote, and vanished. The next night
It came again with a great awakening light,
And showed the names whom the love of God had blessed,
And, lo! Ermyn Orvella's name led all the rest!

SECTION IV
Law

1. The O.J. Simpson Murder Case

As politics in Barbados continues in a state of flux and as all three parties are thinking of ways to ditch their bath-waters (present leaders) and keep the babies (principles and integrity), this article will deal with a more exciting subject – namely, the plight of O.J. Simpson.

The Simpson tragedy contains all the hallmarks of a best-seller novel. There is provocative sex, money, (lots of it), fame, domestic violence and to cap it all – violence.

Just think what Agatha Christie could have done with such real life plots and don't forget the 'whodunnit' aspect of the case. The late Alfred Hitchcock would have taken the above-mentioned ingredients, internalize them and then given us a suspense thriller more gripping than "Birds".

This "O.J." saga confirms that old adage "Truth is stranger than fiction." If the evidence spelled out so far in a Los Angeles courtroom is true, then we have no further need of fiction.

This article will try to objectively analyze four (4) spell-bound aspects of the "O.J." case. Those aspects are (1) race, (2) celebrity status, (3) domestic violence and (4) American Jurisprudence.

The Racial Aspect

In spite of the lip service Americans pay to being a color-blind, multi-racial, multi-cultural society, the whole place reeks of prejudice, select justice and an uncontained eagerness never to give their racial minorities the benefit of any doubt. This is so, whether the minorities be Afro-Americans, Hispanics or Native Americans.

Racism is so rampant and pervasive, that it permeates all strata of society and like outstretched tentacles lay waiting to see who it could grip in its deadly grasp. Racism, indeed is the Achilles heel of American society and successful Blacks who sometimes forget this, pay dearly for their amnesia when they fall from grace.

Ellis Cose, a prominent Afro-American columnist in the July 9, 1994 edition of Newsweek wrote the following about O.J. Simpson: "He (O.J. Simpson)....who tried to slip out of his place, but who was finally forced back in." Author Cose went on to say that "Simpson dressed White, talked White and even married White." Yes there is a lot of empathy for "O.J." in the Black community, but this would have been even greater had he not committed the above-mentioned slights to his race.

Yes, Simpson will get a fair trial in California, not because he is Black, but rather because he is rich and famous. With his money, he has the best lawyers that money could buy.

His Celebrity Status

Yes, like Michael Jackson, "O.J." is a celebrity and his case is drawing a lot of attention: not because he is Black but because he is a celebrity who made it. Someone once wrote, "Those whom the gods will destroy, they first made mad." That's a beautiful metaphor and sounds like one that could be applied to some Caribbean leaders.

The status of being a celebrity is a very fickle and fleeting one. The attempts to blemish and pull down certain Afro-American celebrities like Michael Jackson and special Envoy-Bill Gray, will confirm this.

If a Caucasian, non-celebrity stood accused of the "O.J." alleged crimes, there would be very little public interest in their heinous crimes. Now if a Black non-celebrity stood accused of the crimes "O.J." stands accused of, that Black would have been bound over, tried and executed by now. Such is the level of justice in America.

Domestic Violence

Yes, this case has all the ingredients of a thriller even the hot, current issue of domestic violence is involved. How could one write a best-seller today and leave out the much talked-about subject of domestic violence?

Yes, to murder one's wife is bad, but to have beaten her first makes one destined for the hottest part of hell. As Kerwin Garner wrote recently in another place "....it is one thing tuh beat ah woman and another thing tuh be a murderer." Domestic violence usually means husbands and paramours abusing wives and lovers. It never means the opposite, namely some bossy wife abusing her sick and timid husband.

In America, even domestic violence cannot be divorced from race. It is almost O.K for a Caucasian husband to hit a Caucasian wife but woe to a Black husband who thinks of doing the same. Many Black women in America are not supporting "O.J." because (1) they said he married outside his race and (2) they said no Black wife would have stayed around for eight beatings.

Barbadians already know how much heat this subject produces just by reading the divergent views of Dawn Morgan and Kerwin Garner in a certain weekly tabloid.

American Jurisprudence

American Jurisprudence, for a change looks good. Sometimes television has its good points and the gavel to gavel coverage by the networks was surely a plus for that part of the media. As one interviewee puts it, "This was a great lesson in civics – not to mention law." The fourth amendment is now better known and understood than before this onslaught of television coverage.

Just imagine the opportunity recently lost in Barbados to give a similar lesson in civics and the constitution, when the 'no-confidence' debate was denied television coverage.

In America the public good was the barometer used to justify the T.V. courtroom coverage whereas the public good was not considered, when T.V. coverage of the 'no-confidence' motion in parliament was denied.

As Barbadians would say "Magistrate Kennedy-Powell has bound over O.J. Simpson to stand trial on double homicide charges. It must not be forgotten that these are allegations only and that "O.J." like every other criminal defendant is presumed innocent until found guilty.

It must be remembered that this case is built solely on circumstantial evidence. So far, there has been no weapon, no motive and no eye-witness. All "O.J." has to do is to sit tight. He literally

C. Alfie Gill

has nothing to prove, as it is the prosecution that must prove his guilt beyond a reasonable doubt.

Now we just have to wait for the trial to begin.

(Prof. C. Alfie Gill is a free-lance journalist who resides in the U.S.A. and from time to time writes on the American scene.

2. O.J. Acquitted, Racism Convicted

This writer believes that there is something called poetic justice. Poetic justice can be likened to a person digging a well for another to fall in, but then falls into the well himself.

So it was with the O. J. Simpson case in Los Angeles, California, which ended in an acquittal. The official jury has spoken and wisely, but the arm-chair jurors will be debating the verdict for a long time to come.

A year ago, this writer wrote on "O. J. Saga" (Nation, August 15, 1994). At that time very few people seemed aware of the case, its complexities and potential ramification. Always, one to correctly identify racism, this writer correctly enunciated racism as one of the three main ingredients of the case. The other two were (a) domestic abuse and (b) Simpson's celebrity status.

The jury should be thanked for its service and the people of Los Angeles should be forever grateful to those jurors, for having the will and the strength of character to repudiate racism and police abuses – such as framing innocent persons and planting incriminating evidence on others.

"Oh how are the mighty fallen, tell it not In Garth" wrote a famous poet.

Yes, the Los Angeles police have been dealt two damaging punches, one in the Rodney King case the other in the Simpson case. If the Los Angeles and other police forces in the U.S.A. shed racism and planting evidence, some good would have come out of the Simpson case.

In analyzing the results of this case, three features stand out. They are (1) racism, (2) unethical police practices and (3) the power of money. These three features will be analyzed in depth and then it will be clearly seen that the jury's verdict was correct, from both a legal and moral standpoint. "Honi soit qui mal y pense" translated means 'Evil be to him who evil thinks'.

Racism

Racism is found whenever one race believes and acts as if it were superior to another. Where a murderer usually kills one or two victims, racism claims millions of victims; hence the act of genocide has its roots in racism. This insidious system (racism) had its origin in the establishment of the slave trade. Hundreds of thousands of slaves died during what is called the "Middle Passage". Millions more died from physical abuse, over-work, starvation and lynchings.

As a result of slavery, many (not all) Caucasian Americans assumed the unjustified air of racial superiority, perpetuated in this little ditty.

"If you are white, you are alright, if you are black, stand back".

Hence, it is notions like these that led a mere high school graduate like Detective Mark Furhman to think that he was superior to a "Johnny Cochran, O.J. Simpson, Dr. Charles Drew or Dr. Martin Luther King, Jr." and on and on. This shows the absurdity and mental sickness of racial thinking.

The Simpson case was overwhelmed by racism from day one. Two young Caucasians had been murdered and someone had to be brought to justice, whether by hook or by crook.

A natural place to begin would be with the spouse of one of the victims. That victim happened to be Caucasian and her spouse Afro-American. Thus the unequal treatment in this case which was fueled by the odious virus of racism. Here enters disgraced Detective Furhman, Caucasian and an avowed racist. It was Detective Furhman who brought racism into the case. This peace officer, sworn to uphold the law, was taped as saying "all Blacks should be put in a barrel and burned".

It was this desire for the genocide of the Black race that inspired the lawyer, (par excellence) Johnny Cochran, to liken Mark Furhman to Hitler. Yet Mr. Cochran is deliberately misinterpreted and branded a racist. This was a supreme example of the pot calling the kettle black (literally and metaphorically).

Mr. Simpson has to be eternally grateful to the greatest living lawyer, Mr. Johnny Cochran, who, thankfully took over from Mr. Robert Shapiro (a Caucasian). After the verdict was rendered, Mr. Shapiro went on television and denounced Mr. Cochran for dealing the race card. Although this was the card that caused Mr. Simpson to be acquitted, one can only conclude that had Mr. Shapiro remained the lead attorney, he would not have played this card and therefore would have contributed to the possible conviction of an innocent man. The gratitude due to Mr. Cochran therefore, becomes unending.

The Jury

The jury in the Simpson case was sequestered for nine months and therefore had time in which to bond well. This explains why the unanimous verdict was rendered so quickly. When a Black jury after carefully weighing the evidence and after finding numerous examples of reasonable doubt, returns the only logical verdict, it is denounced as racist. If the jury rendered a verdict contrary to the evidence, then it would be non-racist. Only 'Alice in Wonderland' could follow this logic (or lack of it).

A comparison of the Simpson verdict with those in other high profile cases will be most revealing.

Rodney King

The first Rodney King trial of the four accused white police officers was moved from South-Central Los Angeles with its big black population, to "Simi Valley" with its predominantly white population. Yet the jury in that case, even after seeing the famous beating tapes acquitted all the officers. No one branded those jurors as **racists.**

Similarly in the "Mendez Brothers" famous murder case, the jury was deadlocked in spite of overwhelming evidence of guilt. Once racism continues to exist in the U.S.A., there would be many more of these contradictory verdicts. Mr. Simpson should be forever grateful to his lead attorney and to the highly intelligent jury which he was fortunate to have.

The Power of Money

Sometimes people decry others for having a lot of money, without stopping to think how better off people would be with money, than without. This writer likes the way Pope John Paul II puts it on October 4, 1995 on his arrival at Newark international Airport. The Godly Pontiff said that "none should be too poor to give and none too rich to receive." These remarks besides being very deep, were timely and appropriate.

If Mr. Simpson were the usual penurious, run-of-the-mill accused that ex-detective Furhman was used to, then Mr. Simpson would be in a jail cell tonight, instead of being at home basking in freedom and lavishing praise on the genius Johnny Cochran.

Thanks to Attorney Cochran and thanks to the unlimited amounts of money possessed by Mr. Simpson, racism met its Waterloo in the O.J. Simpson trial. It is therefore, not surprising that Mr. Denny, the white truck driver, beaten in the Rodney king riots, has Mr. Cochran as his attorney. That is the way it should always be. One should be hired for one's ability to do a job and not for one's color.

If Mr. Simpson didn't have money, then his dream defense team could not have hired all the investigators and experts that helped to unravel the prosecution's tainted and very weak case. It was the discovery of the Furhman tapes by investigators, hired by the savvy Johnny Cochran that unmasked Mark Furhman leading to Furhman invoking his Fifth Amendment privileges against self-incrimination.

If Attorney F. Lee Bailey or Attorney Shapiro had done this, they would have been branded as legal genii, not racist. "Words have lost their meanings," protested Alice (in Lewis Carrol's famous work – Alice in Wonderland). It was having money that helped the Simpson dream team to hire the best of experts like Dr. Baden (Medical Examiner) and the great Dr. Lee (D.N.A. expert) who helped to deliver the coup-de-grace to the weak prosecution case, riddled with its abundance of reasonable doubt.

It is therefore, not surprising that the attentive and highly intelligent jury was able to find sufficient reasonable doubt in the prosecution's case and therefore, rendered the only verdict possible – "Not Guilty" – on all counts. Instead of the jury's verdict being attacked, it should be applauded.

The U.S.A. is a great country and could even be greater, if many of its population could drop their childish, meritless beliefs in racial superiority. It is said that "man is made in the image of God" (Genesis 1:26). Therefore, no one image of God could be superior to another.

3. Judges Of Whom We Can Be Proud

Article No. 3

There have been four important court cases in 1992 dealing with the Rule of Law. In three of these cases (all in the Caribbean) the much celebrated 'rule' was upheld. In the other case (in the U.S.A.) the 'rule' was conspicuously flouted.

Citizens invariably ask what is meant by "The Rule of Law". "The Rule of Law" may be defined as the prevalence of law (Lex, Latin) over mere 'arbitrariness'.

Observance of "The Rule of Law" is the surest sign, the highest 'imprimatur' of a democratic, civilized and law-abiding community.

An objective analysis of these now famous four decisions will follow, exemplifying how to observe "The Rule of Law" and in the U. S. case, how not to observe it.

Case No. 1

The first case comes from that paragon of law-abiding nations – namely, Barbados. Earlier in the year, because of the high incidence of crime and the exploits of the renown and now infamous jail escapees; there was a 'fortissimo' and almost universal call for the prompt execution of two condemned murderers (Bradshaw and Hall); but the High Court of Barbados did itself well in refusing to yield to mass hysteria precept known as "The Rule of Law".

Barbados should be proud of itself and feel honored to have judges of such high integrity who preferred to preserve the integrity of the judiciary and "The Rule of Law" than to yield to popular demands for speedy executions.

Years ago, in a certain newly independent African nation, the Chief Justice was removed because he rendered a decision that was not pleasing to that African Leader who held visions of grandeur and infallibility. The act of removing that country's Chief Justice with its concomitant coercion of the court is an excellent example of how not to uphold "The Rule of Law".

The High Court of Barbados rendered its fearless and impeccable prohibition with no attending consequences or fear of consequences. That is how to uphold "The Rule of Law" and that is why the decisions in these two cases were chosen as examples of how to uphold "The Rule of Law" and 'how not to'.

Case No. 2

The next case in which "The Rule of Law" was upheld, comes from the neighboring Independent Republic of Trinidad and Tobago.

In this case Mr. Justice Clebert Brooks rendered a brilliant, fearless, Solomonic decision freeing the Muslimeen detainees in Trinidad for their roles in the attempted coup and failed revolution in 1991. Again the bulk of public opinion and the sentiments of the N.R.C. government favored an opposite decision. Justice Brooks to his credit, preferred to uphold "The Rule of Law" and do what was legally right as opposed to doing what was popular, even if legally wrong.

Instead of miscellaneous invectives and uncalled-for opprobria being meted out to this distinguished jurist, he should be receiving the highest accolades which his country and profession could bestow. The West Indies are indeed fortunate to have such fearless, independent-minded jurists who are not afraid to render justice "though the heavens shall fall" (with apologies to another newspaper) Messrs. Husbands, Moe and Smith (Sir Frederick), the world-wide legal profession salutes you; and the fledgling West Indian Nations should count themselves lucky to have sitting as justices, persons of such fearless high integrity, who refuse to sacrifice "The Rule of Law" on the altar of expediency.

"The Rule of Law" is a product of 'jus naturale' (natural law) and thus in upholding "The Rule of Law" in the above mentioned cases, those judges have also been true to the principles of 'natural law'.

Case No. 3

In the third case, in which "The Rule of Law" was upheld, also comes from that island bastion of justice – Barbados. In this case, that distinguished legal scholar and the then Chief Justice of Barbados, Sir Denys Williams rendered another 'Solomonic' decision when he held in the 'corporal punishment' appeal case that it was unlawful and therefore unconstitutional, to administer court-ordered floggings.

This fearless Chief Justice, without paying any attention to public opinion, held that "The 1966 Barbados Constitution left intact a 1964 ban on court-ordered floggings". He went on to emphasize that the 1966 Barbados Constitution also "banned inhuman and degrading punishment". No words can better describe the above decision than those of Portia in Shakespeare's "Merchant of Venice". "A Solomon has come to judgement". Sir Denys, the worldwide legal profession salutes you and applaud your judicial fearlessness and dedication to 'The Rule of Law'.

Case No. 4

As to the fourth and last case, it is rather an example of how not to honor "The Rule of Law" and comes from that giant to the north, namely the U.S.A. In a now famous (or rather infamous) decision, the U. S. Supreme Court held in the case of Dr. Marchais (Mexican national) that it was not unconstitutional for U.S. agents to invade the territory of a friendly nation and kidnap one of its nationals and bring him illegally into the U.S.A. and before the U.S. courts. If ever justice was ever blind-folded, if a decision was ever sacrificed on the altar of political expediency, this was it. This decision, this miscarriage of justice; sure rivals the African action quoted above. In the African decision, the judge acted correctly, but the country's leader nullified his decision. In the Marchais decision, the U.S. Supreme Court Justices anxious to please, bent "The Rule of Law".

What is the lesson to be learned from these cases? The lesson to be learned is "that it is better to obey ("The Rule of Law") than to sacrifice". The twenty first century is quickly approaching and

West Indian leaders should be about the task of nation building. This entails preserving the best of West Indian traditions and if copy we must, then copy only the best from foreign cultures and traditions. The U.S.A is a great country, but everything American is not worth copying, in particular, its breach of "The Rule of Law".

What makes the U.S.A. decision even more pitiable, is to see the court's only Afro-American Justice, Clarence Thomas concur in this act of lawlessness. (See the N.Y. Times for even stronger sentiments on this heinous decision).

Third world countries should be mindful that U.S.A. agents feel that they have the law on their side and therefore empowered to repeat these acts of lawlessness. As a matter of fact, there have been three attempts by U.S.A. bounty hunters to kidnap and take back to the U.S.A. three Jamaican nationals. One such attempt was thwarted in Jamaica at the airport by security agents of that country. Barbados be vigilant! Justices of Barbados and Trinidad, the international community salutes you for upholding "The Rule of Law" in your respective countries. Your great decisions have proved that the West Indies is ready to have its own final court of appeal.

4. How Best To Eradicate Crime

OPINION

Crime is a social disease and an epidemic of crime is an indication that all is not well with the body 'Social'. Just as sickness is an indication that all is not well with the 'physical' body, we need to take the same holistic approach to crime.

It is accepted that crime is a 'social disease', then as with physical disease, we should first try to identify its cause, and after that, as with A.I.D.S. we should be trying to discover a cure. To find a cure, we need the active help and participation of all the races, classes and institutions. Those institutions to be included are: the church, the school, the community and the home.

The writer will first like to identify what he considers as the root causes of the current crime wave and in doing so, the writer hopes to upset some commonly held notions about the causes of the current crime wave.

The writer on his trips to the beloved isle of his birth has observed that there are two or more Barbados, not just one. There is the Barbados of the upper and middle classes known for their things British: such as cricket, afternoon tea, the B.B.C. and other British idiosyncrasies.

On the other hand, the more dominant lower and poorer classes eschew things British, travel by the mini buses and 'ZR' vans and who prefer things foreign – (Jamaican and Afro-American) like: rap (Dub) reggae, basketball and soccer and the writer's observation is that "ne'er the twain shall meet".

To understand this fact as well as the total feeling of being left out, felt by the predominantly lower classes, is to begin to understand the present social unrest. First. This writer believes that Barbados is too small to have all these classes and divisive sub-groupings. The Founders of the Democratic Labor Party (of which this writer was one) had in mind a more egalitarian, more humane and less divisive Barbados.

The next cause of the social unrest now sweeping the island is the decline in power and influence of the church, the school and the home.

Churches have lost their influence because they have come to be regarded as places to go for a Sunday fix and are not interested in the whole person - that is both body and spirit. Churches can regain their influence, when they also become dispensers of Day Care services, Senior Citizen out-reach programs and after-school and recreational activities for young people.

Next, homes have lost the influence that they formerly wielded. Parents have become younger and in many cases are more poorly educated than did their parents. Today, among the poorer classes, children are literally having children. This however, is a worldwide phenomenon and needs to be addressed on an international level. When people feel empowered and do not feel positively left out, they will respond and do not feel the urge to commit unsocial acts in order to get attention.

Next, the Schools too have lost their influence. The School like the home has lost its influence and cannot remain unblemished when the rest of society is becoming soiled and blemished. Schools are but surrogate homes. Bring back good, wholesome homes and we shall again have schools with influence and which again dispense learning.

This step by step analytical approach to the causes of crime now sweeping our beautiful isle, identifies as the main cause of crime. 1) The feeling of alienation by the lower masses and (2) this taking place at the same time when the foundation of institutions became weakened and less influential. Bring back good homes, good schools and holistically caring churches and we shall have an almost crime-free Barbadian society.

These include an importation and imitation of the most negative features of foreign cultures and sub-cultures. The main ones imitated are Rastafarianism from Jamaica and some of the antics of the

Afro-American sub-culture. Let me uncategorically say that both of the above have very positive, enviable features but have, as usual, negative features, which are easier to copy than the positive ones. If Barbadians must imitate, then let them imitate the best, not the worst, from foreign cultures.

Next there is a preoccupation with things American, like violence-filled television, an idolatrous worship of material things and an inhuman, reckless disregard for the weaker members of society. There is a saying in progressive circles in the U.S.A., namely, "to imitate America is to be like America."

How can Barbadians reduce or eliminate some of the secondary causes of crimes?

(1) If Barbadians must imitate, then let them accentuate the best and not the worst aspects of foreign lands; in other words, imitate the music, clothes and hair styles but not the violence.

(2) To develop a Barbadian personality, a national spirit that will identify and distinguish Barbadians from say: Jamaicans, Brixtonians or Afro-Americans. When visitors come to Barbados, they want to see Barbados, not another Soweto, Harlem or Ladbroke Grove.

Unleash that spirit of creativity, emphasize things Barbadian, empower the masses of Afro-Barbadians, encourage them (not always blame and condemn them) and you will see how fast crime will begin to disappear from our "island in the sun".

To those who would criticize or challenge the above, I offer the following: The United States and the foreign countries with the most crimes and violence are those with the greatest disparities in wealth and injustices; such as southern states like Florida and countries with the greatest record of injustices and alienation of citizens, such as South Africa.

Countries with the highest standard of living and social harmony are those with a high degree of homogeneity, classlessness and inclusiveness such as Japan and the Scandinavian countries. That is the way to reduce crime; that is the way to empower people; that is the way to prevent people from feeling alienated. Start a Barbadian equivalent of the peace corps, which our young people can join and perform services for the poor, the sick, the toddlers and the very old.

Young, poor Barbadians are our greatest source of untapped strength and they are dying; not to commit crimes, but to feel included and to be given a chance to prove too that they are Barbadians. The way to reduce crime is not only to preach sermons, write negative letters to the press; nor to whip them nor hang them. Again Florida and South Africa with the highest number of executions have the highest number of murders world-wide.

Show me a less class-divided, more just and inclusive Barbados and I shall show you a less crime-ridden Barbados.

A Constitutional Crisis In Barbados (1994)

The prime minister has spoken; the home-grown experts and armchair critics have spoken, and so soon will the electorate of a tempestuous Barbados.

Politics is not an abstract science like statistics, rather it is a living, fallible and dynamic science that never ceases to surprise.

This writer will like to analyze the recent constitutional crisis in Barbados (Little England), to see where things went wrong and then conceptualize how (big) England would have handled it.

The Westminster model will only work in a truly democratic society, with a very sophisticated and highly literate populace. So, what went wrong in Barbados? It is easier to quote imported conventions and copy-cat formalistic rituals than it is to breathe the true spirit of Westminster.

It is easy to assign blame and in the recent engineered and well-orchestrated crisis; there was surely a superfluity of blame to pass around.

Was the Prime minister a Victim?

The first role to be analyzed will be that of one of Barbados foremost prime ministers, namely, the right Hon. Lloyd Erskine Sandiford. Prime Minister Sandiford with the help of the I.M.F. had just arrested the economic decline in Barbados and again had his island nation pointed in the direction of stability and renewed economic growth.

From the time he (Sandiford) assumed premiership, some local pundits and naysayers started to predict a rough road ahead for him so a lot of what has taken place could be described as prophets trying to make their prophesies come true. The more the Prime Minister achieved, the less thanks and praise he received. This inexplicable fact helped, no doubt, to shape and produce the psyche that motivated him to advise the Governor General to dissolve parliament and call for a new general election.

One got the feeling that this was not a decision he lightly made, rather it was the culmination of days of prayer, agonizing and soul-searching; all done with the best interest of his party (the D.L.P.) and his beloved Barbados. As one philosopher succinctly said: "It is easier to destroy a house than to build one."

As Barbadians from the Diaspora in unbelief watched events unfold, one could not but help remembering the late Neville Chamberlain of Munich fame, who resigned in disgrace as the then M.P.'S. shouted, "You have held on far too long, in the name of God, go!"

Why Did the Impasse Arise?

One could almost hear a similar cry emanating from a Barbados divided House of Assembly. There was one major difference between Chamberlain and a crushed, heart-broken Sandiford many Barbadians opined and it was this: Chamberlain deserved his fate, but not the unsung Erskine Sandiford. Like Wes Hall and before him Thomas A. Beckett, Sandiford too could say "Had I served my God half as well as I have served my party, in the evening of my life, I would not have come to this." (infamy) This writer feels that history will be kinder to Sandi than many of his critics have been.

Of course the Prime Minister made some mistakes, but they were always mistakes of the heart and never of the head. Should he have called for an election at this time rather than simply step aside? The decision was his and his alone.

For right or wrong, it was his decision. He has to live with that decision and so too must the volatile electorate of Barbados. Throughout the world, Barbadians are renowned for their wisdom and common sense. Barbadians may go near to the brink – that is throwing out the D.L.P. – but when they see what is on the other side, they will shudder and retreat.

On the other side they will see an unpredictable, untried, inexperienced, barely-supported leader of the opposing B.L.P. When thinking, intelligent Barbadians see this, they will quickly stop flirting with the idea of deposing the greatest party that Barbados has ever seen. For it was the D.L.P. under the saintly Errol Walton Barrow who catapulted Barbados from the doldrums of poverty and low economic growth. Sure, Sandiford made mistakes, but at no time has he or his party turned their backs on their beloved fellow citizens.

How The British Does Things

The impasse in the governing party (D.L.P.) arose because the parliamentary system as the British know it, completely broke down. When an invincible force meets an unmovable object, something has to give.

Neither the Prime Minister nor the dissidents wanted to give an iota and something had to give. But did it mean throwing out the baby with the bath-water? (Here the D.L.P. is the baby and Sandiford, the bath-water.) A look at how the British political parties handle analogous situations will prove very enlightening.

On two occasions during Her Majesty's reign, similar situations arose and acting on advice from her privy councilors, Her Majesty named a new prime minister and did not dissolve parliament.

The first occasion was that of the Suez crisis and debacle. The Egyptians had just overthrown King Farouk and then seized the Suez Canal from the British and French. The Americans, on that occasion, acted wisely and refused to support her usual two allies. The British and French were defeated and the House of Commons wanted the head of (then) Sir Anthony Eden, the Tory Prime Minister. Sir Anthony was then fired in the usual British euphemistic manner – that is resigning, claiming serious illness.

Hon. R. A. Butler, the deputy Tory leader was the logical choice to succeed Sir Anthony, but this was not to be. Butler held dome liberal views and this fact caused many in the Tory hierarchy to oppose the elevation of R.A. Butler. The long knives were pulled out and after re-sheathed, Harold McMillan emerged as Prime Minister.

Then history repeated itself a second time. After the Profumo scandal broke, the Tory parliamentary M.P.'s met and again rejected R. A. Butler, choosing as their leader, a man who was not even a member of the House of Commons, namely Lord Alec Home.

Yes, this really happened. In 1964, the British had a Prime Minister who was not even a member of the House of Commons. The lesson here however was the fact that it was the Tory <u>Parliamentary Party</u> making these awful decisions and then informing Her Majesty of them.

The Parliamentary Party Chooses The Prime Minister

Thus, if Barbados was truly imitating the Westminster model, the parliamentary members of the governing party would have stripped their Primer Inter Pares (first among equals) of that title and named a new Primer Inter Pares. Under the British system, it is the parliamentary party that names a Prime Minister and not a general council.

Why this did not happen in Barbados is for the members of the parliamentary D.L.P. to inform the public. At least imitating the British on this occasion could have prevented the present unwanted fiasco.

Conclusion

Where do the parties go from here? It is quite obvious that all is not well in both major parties, because at the height of the local crisis, a parliamentary member of the opposition party went A.W.O.L. (absent without leave).

Both parties have to put their houses in order. Both have to stop washing dirty linen in public and above all, both have to elect the right leaders for the right reasons.

Once the Democratic Labor Party does this, then their members can heal the wounds, close the ranks and go out and win the next election. At this point in its history, Barbadians cannot afford to desert the only party that truly tried to serve all Barbadians.

Finally, Barbadians should be reminded of these words from Shakespeare.

"Those friends whom thou hast and their adoption tried,

Grapple them to thy souls with hoops of steel."

(Prof. Gill who resides in New York is a free-lance journalist who writes sometimes on the local political scene.)

SECTION V

Politics

1. Let The U.S.A. Shelter The Haitians

1987

In crisis what is termed the Haitian crisis, two separate issues predominate. The first is the Haitian refugee crisis and the other is the call for an invasion of Haiti itself.

The United States of America is a great country. Without doubt it is the world's richest and most powerful nation; but in the area of foreign affairs, it sometimes behaves as a mere neophyte.

The United States throughout its history has been a beacon of freedom and its statue of liberty has always stood with outstretched arms to welcome "the wretched, huddled masses of the world's poor." At the turn of the twentieth century, those huddled masses consisted first of Italians, then later Irish and other Europeans. So much so that this phalanx of refugees were referred as WOPs. That is "immigrants without passports." Actually they did have a passport, namely their white skin color. It is this passport that the Haitians lack. The white Cubans of the Mariel boat-lift had it; but the immigrants of the world's oldest Black republic lacked it.

It is this fact that the West Indian leaders need to learn. If they did, then they would be less eager to let the United States off the hook and allow it to continue to practice its uneven immigration policy.

Refugees of the former communist bloc have no difficulty in gaining political asylum. European Jews and white Cubans have no problem in gaining admission. Cubans in leaky boats were not turned back at high seas until recently.

The United States of America must mature and behave like a world power. It cannot be heard to say, "If you are White you're alright, but if you are Black stand back."

When West Indian islands like Jamaica, Antigua and Domenica decide to accept Haitian refugees, they are unwittingly helping the Americans to continue their uneven immigration policies. Barbados is to be commended for not getting involved in the bartering away of refugees' rights, no matter how attractive the temptation and monetary rewards.

2. Should The U.S. Invade Haiti?

1987

Many individuals in the Caribbean and elsewhere have called for an invasion of the sovereign independent country of Haiti (nee St. Germain). Even the Security Council of the United Nations has joined this unholy act.

As the shadow Foreign Secretary of Jamaica (Mr. Hector Wynter) has rightly said he did not observe any breach of international law nor violation of the peace by Haiti. This is another pre-requisites, which would justify an invasion. (Ex post facto).

Haiti has a 'DeFacto' government which has friendly relations with all members of the United Nations. So far no nation has broken off relations with Haiti. This is another pre-requisite to an invasion under international law. One does not invade a friendly country and neither can neighboring states issue invitations to other countries to invade.

For argument sake, suppose Barbados had a fictional prime minister who lost a vote of no-confidence and who would not resign nor call an immediate election, would Barbadians favor the United States or some other country coming to topple the 'De Facto' government of Barbados?

Most Barbadians would answer in the negative. Just like the Haitians, Barbadians would like sovereignty more than they detested their fictional 'De Facto' government. As Barbadians would say, "Let the shoe fit."

This writer is in favor of the removal of the Haitian dictators by the Haitians themselves, assisted by international sanctions. As Mr. Wynter of Jamaica pointed out, he never heard of any such calls to go in and topple the apartheid rulers of South Africa. It must not be forgotten, that then President Reagan of the USA instead of calling for the use of force in South Africa called for something called "constructive disengagement", or as Winston Churchill wisely said, "it is better to jaw-jaw (talk), than war-war (fight).

Some people would point to the Grenadian precedent, but that one is of doubtful legality. If the end justifies the means, then the act of removing those usurpers (Coard, Hudson et al) was justified. Even in Grenada (this writer feels) Grenadians would have made it impossible for the Coard bunch to govern.

Likewise, when the Haitian people themselves have had enough, they would topple the generals. Didn't the Haitians themselves topple 'Baby Doc"?

Similarly, the Filipinos themselves were the ones that put an end to the hated Marcos regime. Likewise it was the residents of the communist bloc countries themselves who put an end to that system. This will always be so, because "right is a greater force than might."

Adherents of the Bible will say "They that live by the sword shall also perish by the sword."

The United States is a great country and a giant super-power. So if the United States want to invade Haiti, the United States is strong enough to do so without token assistance of Barbados and other Caribbean states. No Barbadian nor Caribbean life should be lost in any such exercise of over-kill.

In the United States, in governing circles, there are three schools of thought. One school would like to topple the generals and preserve the status quo, but not restore President Aristide.

Another school would prefer to topple the generals and restore President Aristide. The third and final school would prefer to do nothing. Right now the school to return President Aristide is in the minority. That is why there has been no invasion.

Life is not always simple; things are not always black and white. Big countries sometimes learn that discretion is the greater part of valor.

In conclusion, the West Indies should not accept any refugees. Let the big, rich United States, with its capacity to accept them, be the one to accept them.

Finally, let the United States (per se) remove the generals, restore Aristide and then invite Barbados and others to police the peace.

3. Why President Bush Lost The U.S. Election

Nov. 1992

In Octo3ber 1992, the author of this article writing in another place, correctly predicted the outcome of the 1992 U.S.A. presidential election.

It was correctly predicted by this writer, the Democratic Bill Clinton would defeat the Republican incumbent, President George H. Walker Bush.

Why did George Bush lose the presidency to the Democratic Party challenger from Arkansas?

President Bush's presidency is a lesson on how to lose an election by honoring promises more in the breach than in the observance. How could a president, who only four years ago had won the White House by capturing forty eight states and a spectacular majority, lose the election?

President Bush was President Reagan's vice-president and while the political mantle fell on President Bush, very little of the magic devolved on him.

Four years earlier, President Bush rode to victory by holding on to the vanishing coat tails of Ronald Reagan, supplemented by Bush's appeal for the Caucasian vote by mentioning the Willie Horton's story. (Willie Horton was an Afro-American given temporary furlough from prison and who raped a young female Caucasian while released). Gov. Michael Dukakis of Massachusetts was the Governor who released Willie Horton. George Bush in 1988, by using the code term 'Willie Horton', was able to win the vote of racists without himself being labelled a racist.

So what went wrong this time? The answer is: what in politics is known as a record.

In 1988 George Bush proudly and boastfully declared "read my lips, no new taxes". The voters read his lips in 1988 and voted Republican and can you guess how they were repaid?

The American electorate was thanklessly repaid with the second largest tax increase in the last fifty years. This time around few people were reading George Bush's lips as they were too busy reading his record.

Bush's record was strewn with broken promises and shattered dreams. Twenty million American jobs had been lost to foreign competitors and there was a whopping almost record-breaking 8% unemployment. This translated into about ten million unemployed workers; and what did George Bush propose for 1993?

Right-wing columnist Michael Kingsley, writing in his "New Republic" said that Bush's 1993 budget proposed 11 (eleven) tax increases and thirty new fees – about $35 billion over five years. So Bush had already broken his "no new taxes" pledge, again.

Yes, one more broken promise and one more nail was driven into the coffin of President George Bush on Election Day 1992. There is an old proverb that is very apt to describe Bush's plight. "You can fool some of the people some of the time; but you cannot fool all the people all the time."

So when the writing appeared on the wall, did President Bush get the message? Not likely. Like the proverbial ostrich, Bush continued to bury his head in the sand.

On Monday October 5, 1992 the U.S. Congress for the first time over-rode one of Bush's vetoes. Both Houses of Congress overrode his veto of the cable television bill. That marked the beginning of the end for George Bush.

Respected N.Y. Post reporter, Marsha Krane writing in the New York Post on October 6, 1992 wrote "for Bush whose previous vetoes had been sustained, the over-ride was viewed as evidence of weakness in an already rocky re-election bid."

Cumulatively, all these signs pointed to the impending defeat of the lack-luster President. In spite of all this, President Bush continued to push for a 'capital gains' tax cut, a cut that would only benefit the rich. The more Bush pushed this issue, the more middle-class and poor votes he lost.

Another strike the voters had against President Bush was Dan Quayle (Vice President) his running mate. Vice President Quayle brought no pluses, but a lot of minuses to the ticket – including his inability to spell the word 'POTATO' correctly.

The pity of all this was that George Bush is a congenial person and far less doctrinaire than his predecessor, Ronald Reagan.

How did Afro-Americans view the re-election of George Bush? They were definitely against it. For 12 years (8 under Reagan and 4 under Bush) minorities were treated with benign neglect. So on Election Day 1992, the minorities reciprocated.

Afro-Americans felt very strongly about the inhuman and cold-hearted, forced repatriation of Haitians to their dreaded homeland. It was also rumored that if re-elected, Bush would have closed all U.S. Embassies in the countries whose population was less than five million. If this had been carried through, there would not even have been one embassy in the entire English-speaking Caribbean.

If George Bush had been re-elected the U.S. economy would have lingered in recession and continued to play havoc with the economies of third world countries, leaving them in the Draconian clutches of the New World power – namely the I.M.F. The new world order could not stand another four years of George Bush.

Next, what were the chances of "on again, off again" billionaire candidate Ross Perot? His chances were always negligible. He received the protest vote or the bulk of the undecideds, but this only amounted to 18%. He took votes equally from George Bush and Bill Clinton. The best thing that could be said for Ross Perot, is that he was spending his own money. He did not spend any of the taxpayers' money (via the Presidential Election Fund). This fund is financed by a $2 check off at tax filing time.

Finally why did the Governor of the state of Arkansas win the U.S. Election?

This writer predicted that Governor Clinton would win the election and be declared the next President of the U.S.A. one month before the election.

Governor Bill Clinton is a lawyer, a successful Democratic governor and former Rhodes Scholar. He is married to another lawyer and liberal, Hilary Clinton. Like the late Lady Bird Johnson and the renown Lady Macbeth, Hilary knows how to help Bill Clinton "screw his courage to the sticking point". (Lady Macbeth in Shakespeare's Macbeth Act I)

Governor Clinton's victory over George Bush will usher in a new day (in a new day) in American politics. Gone will be the sole concern of the wealthy and reborn will be the love and empathy for the masses. Clinton's election will see a softening of the harsh Friedmaneque laissez-faire policies pursued during the last twelve years (eight under Reagan and four under the affable but unsuccessful George Bush).

Governor Clinton has articulated sound flawless economic proposals to get the economy moving again and putting Americans back to work. These proposals will help to end one of the longest lasting recessions. This will be good news in third-world countries whose economies were also slowed down because of the U.S. recession.

What is the verdict of the minority community on Governor Clinton? Afro-Americans, for one, were not over-enamored with Governor Clinton. They did not like the silent treatment meted out to the charismatic Jesse Jackson nor the way their community was cold-shouldered in Clinton's attempt to win back the blue-collar Reaganite Democrats.

This might have made good sense from Clinton's point of view, but it will also meant that he will have to mend fences with the Afro-American community after the election. Governor Clinton's victory in the debates and his having a far superior running-mate in Senator Albert Gore, helped seal Governor Clinton's election bid.

What lessons could other countries learn from the grueling election? The main lesson to be learned is that the sure way to defeat, is not to deliver on election promises.

President George Bush promised "No New Taxes" and went on to deliver the second highest tax increase in most people's lifetime. He sowed the wind (of broken promises) and on November 3, 1992 he reaped the whirlwind (of defeat).

Bush failed to communicate his having a vision for America and seemed to be out of touch with the American electorate. On the other hand, Clinton exuded confidence. He behaved with dignity, stuck to the issues and avoided the puerile name-calling indulged in by President Bush and Dan Quayle.

Liberalism is not dead. The P.N.M.s victory in Trinidad, the P.P.P.'s in Guyana, Ingraham's victory in the Bahamas and Governor Clinton's victory in the U.S.A. are proof that voters would prefer government tempered with compassion to the failed, harsh theory known as "Trickle Down".

Governor Clinton, the whole world salutes you, and Third-World countries (like Barbados) can again look forward to good times and renewed prosperity.

4. Celebrating The Closing Of The Embassies

Dec. 1992

(And The Millions To Be Saved)

This writer in his last article made a strong case for the CARICOM Nations to integrate their foreign policies and to be represented overseas by a single ambassador. There are many arguments favoring this step, but one of the main ones, is that of the millions to be saved by closing all the superfluous embassies and consulates.

The present situation is akin to the "Barbados Landship"; that is 'a lot of chiefs and very few Indians,' to use an American metaphor. The following satirical piece (the author hopes) will persuade the CARICOM leaders to take a serious look at uniting the foreign ministries and saving these impoverished islands, millions of badly-needed dollars.

SCRIPT

The scene takes place in Harry's liquor shop with Greiner Blow-Hard and Lick-Mout' Sue as the main characters. There is also one bar maid.

Greiner: "Did any of you read the professor's column last week?"

Blow: "He really wrote a mouthful dah time."

Sue: (With apologies to Lick-Mout Sue) "I agree wid he. I could never understand why a handful of islands and no resources need all o' dem ambassadors. If big China only got one ambassador, by dat reckoning de West Indies shouldn't even have one."

Greiner: "Okay Sue, give somebody a say" (Drinks poured).

Blow: I could think of a million reasons why we should federate and close dem embassies and pocketing the savings is on top o' de list.

Sue:	Federation is the answer, but dat is too easy a solution fuh we leaders to think about".
Blow:	"All dey ever think about is 'where are we going to put the capital and who is going to be prime minister'?"
Greiner:	You are all too pessimistic. You all know dat Bajans is like de British, we are not easy to get along wid."
Sue:	"All I know is dat Buhbadus is broke and like de professuh say, we could save a lot by closing down dem useless embassies".
Greiner:	"Now yuh all give me one good reason why little places like Bar-Bay-Dus should have an ambassaduh to China or to Japan?"
Blow:	Well I can't think of a reason why Nevis or Anguilla should have ambassadors to Finland or Saudi Arabia or places like dat."
Sue:	"Like I keep saying, all I can think of is all de money to be saved when we close all those useless, expensive embassies and consulates."
Greiner:	"And don't fuhget de Mercedes Benz, de Linciln Continentals and de Rolls Royces that won't be needed."
Blow:	"No doubt de islands broke, de money keep going up in smoke and de leaders can't see it."
Sue:	"Now if Buhbadus close all its embassies where would we send Jaycee next?"
Greiner:	"To keep Jaycee as an ambassador is no good reason to go in for all the expense involved in keeping all those embassies." (Drinks poured)
Sue:	"If you close all dem embassies, we are going to lose a lot 'o fun."
Greiner:	"What kind of fun?"
Sue:	Don't you wise guys remember dat time when Buhbadus had an ambassador to the U.N. and he kept some noisy dog dat de people in de Bronx threatened to shoot?"
Blow:	"Oh yes, and de ambassador came out and say 'if yuh shoot he dog, dat will create an international incident."

	(mockingly, loud laughter and each gives the other a high five).
Sue:	"I always wondered wuh de goodly gentleman meant by dat. Was Buhbadus going to launch a nuclear attack against the U.S?' (Loud laughter)
Greiner:	(Impatiently) "I can't stand you Bajans, yuh always want to make fun o' serious tings."
Blow:	"Come on man, you know you enjoying it."
Sue:	"Gee, I thought you wuz de one who once wuz telling we 'bout what a press officer does.
Blow:	"Come on Gee, I didn't hear it, so tell us one more time."
Greiner:	It goes like dis. I had dis friend who told me he had a big job in some embassy. So I asked him what he did."
Blow:	"What did he say?"
Greiner:	He said he was the press officer. So I asked him what did a press officer do? He said that his job was to read the leading papers in that country and wherever he saw the name of his island, he was to cut it out." (They looked at each other curiously)
Sue:	"Gee man, there was more to it than that."
Greiner:	(Getting angry) "I am coming to it if you let me."
Sue:	"Okay Gee."
Greiner:	"Well my friend, the press officer said that once a whole year went by and he didn't have anything to cut out."

(Laughter.)

Blow:	"And dat is de kind of nonsense we have to pay for."
Greiner:	I really could tell you all agree with the professor and feel that uniting the foreign ministries and having one ambassador for the whole of CARICOM would be a good idea."
Sue:	"Now tell me what secrets St. Kitts or Nevis have to send home." (Laughter)

Greiner:	"At least those diplomatic pouches will not be floating around anymore."
Sue:	"And de dope pushers would have to find some other way to smuggle in their dope."
Blow:	"I never even thought o' dat. Dat is even one more reason we don't need all those useless embassies." (All nod in agreement.)
Greiner:	"Now let me see all who agree that without any more cuhdoo, de islands should integrate their foreign policies and be represented by one ambassador only."

(All raise their glasses and say, "Agreed.")

All:	"Agreed!" (Clink) "Agreed!"
Greiner:	(To barmaid) "One fuh de road fuh everybody."
Blow:	(With glass raised) "To us."
Greiner:	"To federation, in the near future." (All drink)
Sue:	(With raised glass and a little unsteadily.) "To uniting our foreign policies," clink of glasses) "And to closing the embassies and saving millions at the same time."

(Final clink of glasses.)
(Calypso music)

5. Reply To U.S. Under-Secretary Of State

June 1992

ARTICLE #6

Dear Under-Secretary,

I almost fell off my chair when I heard that you issued an "Advisory" to your citizens cautioning them about going to Barbados because of the rising incidence of crime there.

Sir, you must have read your statistics wrong and got your countries mixed up. Barbados a crime-ridden country and the U.S.A. a peace-loving one? In that case sir, I dismiss your "Advisory" as either a piece of fiction or a product of a hallucinogenic mind.

A friend of mine has asked me to tell you that you wouldn't know a peaceful country since you never lived in one. Sir, more than 25 Barbadians have been murdered in your crime-free country this year, including one enjoying the sanctity and security of one of your high schools in New York City, less than two months ago.

Yes, I know what you will say, "Three murders in two months in the same school can't be that bad. It could have been much worse. More than that, they were only children of minorities who would have grown up to be bad anyhow."

Let us examine a few facts. More New Yorkers are killed in a single day than Barbadians killed in Barbados in a whole year. Not only Barbadians but other foreign nationals are slaughtered whole-sale in your peaceful country. CANA NEWS in a Press Release of April 10, 1992, reporting in CaribNews (NYC) of the week ending April 14, 1992, said that over 20 Belizians were slaughtered in just six (6) months.

Shall I go on Sir? More Jamaicans are killed in your country in a month than are killed in Jamaica in a whole year. I understand that one of your fellow under-secretaries has said that Haitians have "one chromosome less for peace and one more for violence. Sir, I have concluded that these two statements (Yours and your colleague's) are no accident but are a deliberate, systematic and paranoiac act to paint two peace-loving countries with the same tar-brush with which you are painted.

Can I remind you of some of the violent acts in your history? First, your country was begat in blood. Your founding fathers did not recommend 'constructive disengagement' from the British; yet this is the course of action which you recommend that South Africans follow.

Violence in your country, Sir, has claimed the lives of some of your presidents. These include Abraham Lincoln who opted for the abolition of slavery and the preservation of the Union as well as president John F. Kennedy who dared to befriend some of his black fellow citizens.

Yes, I know you will say that minorities commit a lot of the crimes in the U.S.A. Yet who murdered John and Robert Kennedy? Who murdered the greatest American that ever lived, the late, saintly Dr. Martin Luther King, Jr. in your crime-free country? Was it a minority person who committed any of these heinous crimes? No Sir, it was always one of your Aryan pure, blue-eyed, lily-white citizens who perpetrated each one of these acts.

Barbados Sir, and the other Caribbean nations can teach your country a thing or two about harmonious race relations. Come to Barbados and get an introductory course in race relations. Have you ever heard of a black policeman clubbing and brutalizing a harmless white citizen? No Sir, our policemen are too civilized, too disciplined, too well-trained to commit such atrocities.

Not only is violence rampant in your country but so also are discrimination and injustice. Your constitution proudly says "all men are created equal" and yet as they signed that document the founding fathers boasted about the number of slaves they held.

Do you remember the famous (rather, infamous) U.S. Supreme Court decision in the Dred Scott Case? That Supreme Court held that "Blacks had no rights that a white man had to respect". Yes and here we are 100 years later with white policemen in Los Angeles, New York, Miami and many other cities feeling the same way.

Mr. Under-Secretary have you ever heard the name "Rodney King"? Yes, I said Rodney King. Yes Mr. King was the U.S. citizen living in Los Angeles who was beaten to a pulp for the world to see. (Thanks to a video camera.)

How was this wanton run-amok violence by police dealt with? Yes, it is true that those four, white sadistic, racist policemen were charged with citizen King's beating. Yes, twelve of their fellow-citizens yes and twelve of yours (lily-white) in true Dred Scott Decision form found those policemen 'Not Guilty.' No Sir, I am not writing about crime-plagued Barbados (according to you). I am writing about the bastion of crimelessness, that paragon of virtue and peace called the United States of America. No Sir, I am not dreaming; then it must be you who are.

Finally, I have two (2) recommendations to make. 1) That all Barbadians, Haitians, Jamaicans and other slandered third-world people should bring class-action suits in the U.S.A. courts and 2) The same slandered nations should now issue their own 'Advisory' warning to their citizens (with justification) about the real risks they run if they misguidedly decide to visit the most crime-ridden country on the face of the earth.

Withdraw your 'Advisory' Sir! Apologize to the offended nations and ask them to help you and your country learn to live in 'Peace and Racial Harmony.'

Respectfully,
Offended Barbadian.

6. To Federate Or To Disintegrate

To federate or not to federate is not the question. Rather, the question should read, to federate or to disintegrate, that is the real question.

The Psalmist wrote "Behold how good and pleasant a thing it is, for brethren to dwell together in unity", but the West Indies have always found more blessedness in a state of disunity.

A short history of the attempt to federate or to confederate will first be in order. Even the choice of name has been inconsistent. In the late 19th century, the nomenclature was confederation, in the fifties (1950's) it was federation and the present murmuring is about something called integration. Whatever it is called, it is surely lacking, as the islands of the former British West Indies sink into deeper obscurity.

THE ATTEMPT TO CONFEDERATE

Confederation in the late 19th century will first be looked at. At that time the British got hold of a quirk (and the British are famous for quirks) for whatever omnipotent reason that besieged them. They suggested that Barbados should confederate with the then Windward Islands.

The plantocracy vehemently opposed this suggestion of (con) federating "Little England' with a bunch of patois-speaking small islands. The masses of Afro-Barbadians decided that confederation had to be good for them since it was so bitterly opposed by the governing class of Caucasian Barbadians. The bottom line is that the masses rose up and rioted for days. The confederation riots as in South Africa, were brutally put down and so ended the talk about 'confederation'.

For the next fifty years or so, there was no further talk of confederation (or coming together).

In the 1930's business was on the decline and the entire western world was in the throes of what came to be known historically as the 'Great Depression'. Suffering in the islands was unbearable and spontaneously island after island stretching from Jamaica in the North to Trinidad in the South, rose up in arms. Again, the riots in the thirties (1930's) were brutally put down, but one good thing resulted; namely, the appointment by the British government of the Moyne commission. The commission was named after its beneficent and impartial chairman, Lord Moyne.

The result of this commission was that the islands were given adult suffrage and for the first time, indigenous leaders from among the masses appeared on the scene. There was Alexander Bustamante in Jamaica, Grantley Adams in Barbados, Julian Marryshaw in Grenada and Captain Capriani and Uriah Butler in Trinidad. It is imperative to know these facts before studying the next attempt at federation in the fifties (1950's).

By the 19550's the former British Empire had started to break up, so the British had yet another hunch or quirk for the West Indies. You guessed correctly if you guessed 'federation'.

The federation of the 1950's was the brain-child of the British, concerned for one primary reason only; namely to administer the ten islands as a unit, with a governor general (British, of course) in charge. This was the kind of federation conceived by the British and swallowed hook line and sinker by the then suppliant West Indian leaders.

Federation was never sold to the masses. To sell a product, a salesman must at least believe in what he is selling. The then West Indian leaders did not conceive the concept of federation and none had a passion for it. The federation of the 1950's was destined to be a failure. Unlike the period of confederation, there were no mass riots. The only interests most of the leaders had, were (1) who was going to be the Prime Minister and (2) which island was going to be the site of the federal capital.

As the delegates-plenipotentiary met at Lancaster House, this writer wrote to them reminding them that the substance of the federal constitution, was of more importance than the shadow - that is the site of the federal capital. That letter appeared both in the Times of London and the other local daily newspaper. Like the late Marryshaw of Grenada, this writer has been one of the most consistent and ardent advocates of federation, which should culminate in the formation of the United States of the Caribbean.

In 1956 the agreement to form a colonial type of federation was signed. Trinidad was selected as the site of the first and last capital of the West Indian federation and the late Sir Grantley Adams of Barbados became the first and last Prime Minister of the federation. In the opinion of this writer, both of those selections were fatal mistakes.

The choice of the second largest unit (island) as the choice of capital was flawed because experience has shown that the site of the capital of the world's most successful federations has always been a smaller unit. Hence Canberra is the capital of Australia and not Sidney. Ottowa is the capital of Canada and not Toronto and these are only two of the many examples. For this reason alone, citing the capital in Trinidad was a geographical error.

Next selecting Grantley Adams to be Prime Minister, some West Indians always felt was a mistake, as he was the most Pro-British and least passionate leader about federation. However, Sir Grantley was the natural choice as Prime Minister as the P.N.P. in Jamaica was defeated in the federal election and Eric Williams newly on the scene, had no interest in the matter.

The rest is history, federation was a one-day wonder and went the way of confederation and the dinosaur. So where does this leave the West Indies, at a time more and bigger integration units are being formed? The impossible has happened in Europe, formerly feuding tribal nations have buried their hatchets and have decided to coalesce into the United States of Europe.

The United States not to be left out, in 1992 formed N.A.F.T.A. consisting of the United States of America, Canada and Spanish-speaking Mexico.

If these disparate countries can come together, why should it be so difficult for the English speaking West Indies to come together; regardless of the nomenclature of the movement?

Separation breeds insularity, disunity and disrespect. Think of the great savings, if instead of having less than four million people represented by ten ambassadors and a countless host of staff-persons and hangers-on; there could be only one ambassador with a fraction of the present astronomically high number of staff persons. This thought alone should have the leaders rushing to integrate. The People's Republic of China with close to a billion people is represented by one ambassador only, at the United Nations, but the English-speaking West Indies with its less than four million citizens is represented by some ten (10) ambassadors. This is what is called overkill, if ever there was such a thing.

What is the hope of the future? The creation of a West Indian spirit also the free movement of goods and people is imperative. A good beginning was made by spreading around the various colleges of the U.W.I; but what is needed now is a set-up, where some high school students will attend school in a neighboring island before graduating, even if but for one semester.

This time the people must be federated, not islands and certainly not the leaders. In order for the United States of Europe to emerge, they first opened up their birders to goods, (the Common Market), next to persons and finally to every aspect of life, including currency. Besides the free movement of goods in CARICOM countries, there must be free movement of persons and the immediate integration of foreign ministries and defense forces.

To this limited beginning other areas can be added later. The advantage of the above approach is that it doesn't add to expenditures, rather it should lead to enormous savings. Just think of all the embassies and consulates Barbados has abroad, think of the badly needed dollars used to run them and then think of those same millions saved, when these same unwanted embassies and consulates are closed forever.

The time for West Indians to come together is <u>now</u>. Today is the day of N.A.F.T.A. and the U.S.E., can the West Indies therefore afford to remain disunited and unfederated? This writer feels the answer is <u>no</u>, and call on West Indians who similarly believe, to take the first steps to integrate, and remember "United we stand, divided we fall".

(Prof. Gill is a free-lance writer who now resides in the U.S.A.)

7. Barbados Too Had Its Crown Heights

1989

As this writer penned his last article on "The Crown Heights Affair," he could not help but recalling the Barbados of yesteryear, with its multiplicity of Crown Heights or its equivalent.

It is said that people who do not remember their history are destined to repeat it. Young Barbadians, therefore, should get to know their Barbadian history. Such history must not only encompass tales about the Portuguese and Lord Nelson, but must empirically include episodes about: Strathclyde, Bellville and Sturges among others.

Why should young Barbadians learn history of a place like Strathclyde and Belleville in St. Michael and of Sturges in St. Thomas?

The answer is: "In order to understand the situation in Crown Heights, New York, Barbadians only have to recall the Bellevilles and Strathclydes of 1930s, 1940s and even the 1950s.

The writer would first like to describe the Strathclyde of his school days in the forties. (1940s).

Strathclyde is an old residential suburb in Bridgetown. It is bounded on the west by Barbarees Hill and on the east by Lower Bank Hall. During the period under recall, Barbados was somewhat like South Africa and the deep South in the U.S.A. with a superfluity of segregated neighborhoods. Yes, apartheid at one time reigned supreme in the green, luscious, tropical isle of Barbados, also known as Little England. To remember Strathclyde is to begin to understand the events of Crown Heights, New York, U.S.A.

Yes, young Barbadians, your precious, ultra-modern paradise of today, once had an area where a row of block stones about two and a half feet high, separated the genteel, quiet, Afro-Barbadians (Blacks) from the (then) more discriminating Caucasian Barbadians (Whites).

This two-and-a-half-foot wall was as much a dividing barrier between Black and White as was the Berlin wall that separated the former East and West Berlin. One's color dictated on which side of the wall one lived and like Crown Heights non-mixing of the races was the order of the day.

Afro-Barbadians could only trespass on the Caucasian side (1) with permission and (2) between the hours of 9a.m and 6 p.m. and never on a Sunday.

To enforce this law of segregation, it is easy to guess who was hired to enforce it. Yes, of course an Afro-Barbadian, referred to in those not too distant days, as "Watchie". In those very (un) enlightened days, there was no time for euphemism like security officer.

Not long ago, one of my friends and I were recalling this former enclave of divisiveness and segregation and started to regale ourselves with anecdotes about formerly segregated Strathclyde.

My home-boy (to use the current lingo) rocked me with his favorite anecdote. My friend said that one Sunday, after Sunday school, he and a friend decided to defile the lily-white section of Strathclyde with their uppity presence. They had no sooner set foot on the dirt of Strathclyde when the "Watchie" grabbed my friend's partner. My friend being fleet of foot, made good his escape and thus avoided getting a criminal record.

Not to be outdone, I gave him my favorite and really true anecdote. My maternal grandmother was a private nurse and at one time took care of the infirm aunt of Rev. Simmons, who was then a vicar at St. Leonard's Anglican Church and who lived in Strathclyde. On grandma's day off, my sister Dolores and I used to go to Strathclyde to escort grandma home. (Remember all this happened in the forties (1940's).

Well every time your writer had to pass water (urinate), you can guess which side he chose to be recipient of the golden and unwanted liquid. Yes, your guess was correct, if you said the Caucasian side. There are stories too numerous to tell about Strathclyde and its dividing and divisive row of block stones. Like the Berlin wall, Strathclyde wall came tumbling down some years ago.

Strathclyde was not the only area like Crown Heights or some suburb Johannesburg. Belleville too, was an area like Strathclyde with its curfew hours and good old "Watchie" to enforce it.

Belleville is also in St. Michael and is more southerly than Strathclyde. Belleville consists of eleven avenues running parallel to each other. On the north is Belmont Road; on the south is Collymore Rock and it is bounded on the east by Pine Road and on the west by the now-famous, George Street.

Again, Afro-Barbadians had to have good reason to set foot on Belleville soil. Usually it would be a case of some Black Bajan woman seeking a position as a servant or some strapping, Black Bajan male seeking a prestigious position as a gardener or chauffeur. Again, no Afro-Barbadian dared to show his or her face in Belleville after sundown. Like the boss slave-driver during slavery, "Watchie" was usually more aggressive in keeping out his own the master; (that is the White Barbadian.)

Again the rule was, from sunrise to sunset, but never on a Sunday. This is similar to Hasidim in New York trying to exclude Gentiles (mainly Blacks) on the Sabbath. On Sundays, White Barbadians wanted to be free from them (that is Black Barbadians).

Yes, there are some humorous anecdotes too, that one can tell about Belleville. My favorite one goes like this: One Sunday, "Watchie" apprehended this beautiful Black Bajan woman, attired in her Sunday best. "Watchie" asked her if she was looking for a job as a maid. The alert young lady replied "No sir, I want to be the first to see which of these lily-white ladies will work for someone like me."

I never found out that lady's name but I shall like to call her the Sojourner Truth of Barbados. (Sojourner Truth was an American runaway slave who led many slaves to freedom, via the under-ground railroad).

Last, but not least, is the area known as Sturges, (after a small plantation in the parish of St. Thomas). St Thomas is one of the two parishes not surrounded by the sea. Sturges became famous (or more infamous), when the son of the Caucasian owner shot an innocent, harmless, angelic little Afro-Barbadian boy just like the Hasidic driver in Crown Heights ran over the little Guyanese Gavin Cato. Not only did Swain (the planter) kill that innocent little boy, but he had the temerity to say that he thought he (Swain) was shooting at a rabbit.

If ever there was a clear-cut case of premeditated murder, this was it. The Caucasian authorities who then ruled the island made sure Swain would not have to face the gallows, by only charging him with manslaughter. To add icing to the cake, his family retained, as his attorney, the then labor leader of the Afro-Barbadian masses.

The bottom line is that Swain received no real punishment. He received a little slap on the wrist; that is, a mere eighteen months in jail for taking this young Barbadian's life. Swain only served part of the sentence, wore his own clothes in jail as well as ate food from his father's home every day he spent at Glendairy prison.

Now I have revealed the Sturges horror, Barbadians can understand the analogy drawn with Crown Heights and Johannesburg, South Africa.

Today in Barbados, nearly all battles have been won, that is probably why today's young Barbadians get into all kinds of mischief. Unlike their parents' young days, there is no divisive wall in Strathclyde or anywhere in the island waiting to be demolished.

Social activism is about dead in Barbados. Complacency has set in and decadence is not far behind. The schools, parents and would-be-leaders must inform the young of the past. This way, like the Jews, Barbadians can make sure it (separation) will never happen again.

8. Letter to the Mayor

June 8, 2005
The Mayor, N.Y.C.
City Hall
New York, NY 10007

Dear Mayor,

   I am a resident of Co-op City, Bronx, New York and a frequent user of the Express Bus service, which New York City is about to take over.

   I work on 125th Street in Manhattan and am daily subjected to great inconvenience and additional expense because the first downtown stop is 84th Street. Passengers waiting to get off at 125th and 116th have to bypass those stops. We must then get on the subway or bus and ride back uptown at additional time and expense.

   Whatever was the original purpose no longer applies. There is significant growth and rebirth of the uptown commercial corridor as well as the residential stock. Today, one can be mugged uptown, but downtown one can be mugged and/or lynched.

   In this election year the Co-op City riders are asking you and the city council to do something about this inconvenience.

Thank you,
C.A. Gill

P.S. Since 2007 BX7 stops in Harlem.

SECTION VI

Adios

Death the Leveller

By James Shirley (1596 – 1666)

1] Death the Leveller by JAMES SHIRLEY (1596 – 1666)
"The glories of our blood and state
Are shadows, not substantial things;
There is no armour against Fate;
Death lays his icy hand on kings:
Sceptre and Crown
Must tumble down,
And in the dust be equal made
With the poor crooked scythe and spade."

2] By Samuel Taylor Coleridge
"To meet, to know, to love – and then to part,
Is the sad state of many, a human heart."

Adieu, Adios, Goodbye,
My Friends, Mes Amis, Mis Amigos

C. Alfie Gill

Printed in the United States
By Bookmasters